GAME OF MY LIFE

CHICAGO

BEARS

GAME OF MY LIFE

CHICAGO

BEARS

MEMORABLE STORIES OF BEARS FOOTBALL

LEW FREEDMAN

SPORTS
PUBLISHING

Sports Publishing books may be purchased in bulk at special discounts for sales promotion, corporate gifts, fund-raising, or educational purposes. Special editions can also be created to specifications. For details, contact the Special Sales Department, Sports Publishing, 307 West 36th Street, 11th Floor, New York, NY 10018 or sportspubbooks@skyhorsepublishing.com.

Sports Publishing® is a registered trademark of Skyhorse Publishing, Inc.®, a Delaware corporation.

Visit our website at www.sportspubbooks.com.

10 9 8 7 6 5 4 3 2 1

Library of Congress Cataloging-in-Publication Data is available on file.

ISBN: 978-1-61321-202-8

Printed in the United States of America

CONTENTS

ACKNOWLEDGMENTS

The author wishes to thank several people for their assistance in providing methods of contacting former members of the Bears player roster.

Special thanks to Chicago Bears senior director of corporate communications Scott Hagel, long-time *Chicago Tribune* pro football writer Don Pierson, long-time *Tribune* sports staffer Fred Mitchell, and the Pro Football Hall of Fame library research staff in Canton, Ohio.

And another thank you to the 28 former players who gave of their time and memories with the stories they told for this book.

INTRODUCTION

A charter franchise of the National Football League, the Chicago Bears are the brainchild of George Halas, who nurtured and supervised the team from the earliest days of professional football.

The Bears are proud possessors of one of the most glorious team histories in the sport, a team that has won more championships (nine) than any other and put more men (26) into the Hall of Fame in Canton, Ohio, than any other.

Halas presided over his Bears as player, head coach, general manager, president and owner for 63 years. His influence contributed greatly to making professional football what it is today—the most popular team sport in America. Whenever football discussions turn to all-time greats and all-time important figures in the game, Halas' is often the first name mentioned.

Over time, the fortunate Bears enjoyed listing some of the most fantastic and memorable players of all-time on their rosters. Red Grange, Bronko Nagurski, Sid Luckman, some of the most famous pro players in history, graced the Bears' gridiron. They are long gone, but many of the players who followed, who played for Halas, who adopted the Bears way, and who injected talents and experiences into Bears lore, made terrific memories for the fans and for themselves.

Time has a way of stealing past us, then accelerating into the distance, dimming achievements. But many Bears stalwarts of the past, who contributed to the 1963 championship victory and the 1985 Super Bowl team—who contributed to the legend of the Bears—take pleasure in recounting their greatest game, their favorite game, their best game.

For some, a game had special meaning because it was their first chance to contribute to the team in their professional career. For others it was a not-to-be repeated individual performance. For others still, the game helped propel their team onward to greatness that season. And for a few it was the thrill of championship-game participation and victory itself.

Different players remember different events in their own way and review the stories in their own minds from a unique perspective. Some were reluctant to toot their own horn and boast about their own sterling day. They wanted to stick to talking about team achievement.

Intriguingly, many players whose careers overlapped with the late Hall of Fame running back Walter Payton, who played for the Bears between 1975 and 1987 after emerging from Jackson State of Mississippi, found themselves talking about his ability, his personality, his all-around football talent, and specific performances. Unfortunately, Payton, who died in 1999 of liver disease, can't speak for himself, so these reminiscences from teammates must stand as testimony to his skill and character. Their words make it clear that they all admired him.

The career of a professional football player is generally brief, the lifespan of a player with a single team often shorter. However, in communities where the sport's tradition is greatest, in places like Chicago, those who saw the players play, those who collected their bubblegum cards, those who consider watching pro football and "Da Bears" as much a part of their organized religion as attending church on Sundays, never forget.

The 28 players who tell the stories of their greatest games and greatest memories, from showdowns with the chief rival, the Green Bay Packers, to the 1963 and 1985 title teams, represent a half-century of Bears history. Being a member of the Chicago Bears was a highlight of their lives. The same might be said for those who watched them, cheered them on, rooted for them to win. The players made names for themselves in Chicago, and Chicago still recalls them fondly.

—Lew Freedman

GAME OF MY LIFE

CHICAGO

BEARS

1

DICK BUTKUS

Mud on the pants, grass stains on the jersey, stubble on the chin, and blood on the nose—even those who never saw Dick Butkus play live carry an image of him in their heads as the most ferocious defensive player who ever terrorized a National Football League opponent. His reputation for toughness, for Mack truck hits, for spilling the guts of enemy running backs, has grown to mythic status. As much as Babe Ruth's stature as home-run hitter has been enhanced by the passage of time, Butkus' stature as the meanest, roughest, most feared linebacker of his generation grows the older he gets.

It has been more than 30 years since Dick Butkus roamed the turf of Wrigley Field and Soldier Field as a magnificent specimen of football defender, a pure havoc wreaker with both strength and speed encapsulated in his 6-foot-3, 245-pound body. But although his career was only nine seasons long and he never played on one of the Bears' nine championship teams, he somehow symbolizes the franchise. Over time, the essence of being a Bear has been distilled to the middle linebacker position. Bill George, Dick Butkus, Mike Singletary, and Brian Urlacher are the quartet of super players who cemented themselves in the role over a 50-year span. From the mid-1950s to the present day, with only minimal interruption, the Bears' favorite son defensive star has been a middle linebacker who could match skills with anyone in the league and regularly was selected for all-star teams.

Each of the four was recognized for his special talents, his leadership, his way of separating foes from their helmets. Yet it seems to many that Butkus hit harder, disrupted teams more, made others tremble more. Other players circled him warily. One day, they were sure, Butkus would hit a runner so hard he would rupture something, kill the man on the field. Yes, they thought, fitting for a Chicago Bear, the man really did have the power of a grizzly.

Brian Urlacher, the present-day holder of the esteemed middle linebacker position in the Bears' lineup, grew up in New Mexico and said he didn't know anything about the Bears when the team drafted him in 1999. Check that—he was aware of one aspect of Bears history.

"I knew Butkus," he said.

Not personally, mind you. He meant by reputation. Yes, even long after Butkus' retirement, word of his prowess was still spreading to the desert Southwest.

Paul Hornung, the Green Bay Packers Hall of Fame halfback, was reminiscing in the *Chicago Tribune* during the 2005 football season and recalled his first and enduring impression of Butkus when the teams played for the first time during Butkus' rookie year in 1965.

Hornung said head coach Vince Lombardi underestimated Butkus, telling Hornung and his fullback companion, Jim Taylor, another all-time great, that they would have an easy time running their trademark sweep on offense.

"Butkus made 27 unassisted tackles," Hornung said. "And Vince apologized saying, 'This guy must be special.' Of course he did turn out to be special. Butkus was the best. He was mean and ornery."

Richard Marvin Butkus was born in Chicago on December 9, 1942. He attended Chicago Vocational High School and the University of Illinois. He was a first-round draft pick of the Bears in 1965 and later that year intercepted five passes for his new team. Butkus recovered 25 fumbles in his career (he either hit runners so

The hardnosed Dick Butkus, who came out of the University of Illinois to star as a middle linebacker for the Bears, is regarded as one of the most ferocious defensive players of all time. Butkus took up acting after retiring from football.
Photo by Diamond Images/Getty Images

hard they bobbled, or he scared them into dropping the pigskin) and was selected all-NFL seven times. The Bears retired his No. 51 jersey, and Butkus was elected to the football Hall of Fame in Canton, Ohio, in 1979.

Butkus' NFL career lasted nine seasons, all in the middle of the Bears defense, but it was cut short by a knee injury, surgery, and subsequent infection. It was a career sadly too short for a legend, and it ended unfortunately. Butkus sued the Bears and doctors for poor medical treatment and received a settlement in 1976. He was estranged from the team for many years.

After his football career ended in 1973, Butkus worked in Hollywood. He did movie and TV work, even appeared on *Wheel of Fortune*, winning nearly $30,000. Butkus was a key figure in the Miller Brewing Company's ads featuring famous sports figures in mini-skits promoting the beer. When the Sylvester Stallone boxing character in the movie *Rocky* named his bulldog "Butkus," somehow it seemed appropriate.

During the fall of 2005 Butkus participated in the making of a reality TV show following the trials of a high school football team in Pennsylvania. Butkus served as the team's coach. He co-authored a 1997 autobiography with writer Pat Smith entitled, *Butkus Flesh and Blood: How I Played The Game*. Butkus lives in Malibu, California, where he also has an insurance company.

Although Butkus visits Chicago frequently, he does not attend Bears games.

"I just watch them on TV," Butkus said.

True to his nature, Butkus worked to stay in top physical shape and occasionally challenged himself with dramatic endurance efforts. One of those exploits harkened back to one of the two games Butkus selected as among the most memorable in his playing career. In the other he played a rare offensive role.

October 24, 1971

BRIGGS (TIGER) STADIUM
CHICAGO BEARS 28 - DETROIT LIONS 23
By Dick Butkus

It was late in the game. Joe Schmidt was their middle linebacker, and there was always a kind of rivalry going between us because he was a very good player. My dealings were with their center, Ed Flanagan, for most of the game. But time was running out, we were winning, and they were throwing desperation passes, trying to hit long ones.

So I was back in pass coverage on one particular play, and I saw this Chuck Hughes (the Lions' 28-year-old wide receiver who was 5-foot-11, 175 pounds) walking back to the huddle. He was deep in our area, like 10 or 15 yards past the line of scrimmage. I could see the color in his face wasn't good. And then he did just a *BOOM*. He fell right on the ground.

In Detroit, like in Wrigley Field, both benches were on the same sidelines. Our doctor and their doctor were on the same side, and I just started signaling for our doctor to come out there. I don't know if I was the first guy who spotted what was wrong because of the pass pattern or whatever. The ball was overthrown—Greg Landry was the quarterback—and Hughes started coming back to their huddle. The way he looked just caught my eye, and then he dropped over.

The doctors were out there and everything and they didn't know quite what it was. But he died. Later, they claimed Hughes had a circulatory system of a 60-something-year-old man. I was near the play, but I didn't hit him or tackle him on it or anything. But when a photograph came out of the doctors running onto the field, I was kind of like standing, looking down at him from a distance. But the angle of this picture that appeared in the paper the next day made it seem like I was closer. Well, somebody sent me a copy of the picture and wrote on it, "Now you did it. You finally did it." Like I finally killed somebody. I remember going back to Detroit for the funeral.

I've had different games to remember, but that was so weird. I had always said that I loved football so much that I wouldn't mind dying on the field, but that made me think.

About three years ago in the summer I was in Las Vegas doing some insurance business, and I had been talking to some people in casinos. Well, I had always wanted to go to Death Valley on the hottest day of the year and work out. I drove there and stayed at Furnace Creek. I was eating, and I asked the waitress, "What's the hottest time of the day?" She said, "Around three o'clock."

So the next morning I swam in the pool, then I went over to the golf course. They were shutting it down around mid-day. I was the last guy on. My feet were bothering me, so I played in my socks. By the 18th green, my feet were burning. I had to run across the blacktop. It was like I was running on hot coals.

It was like 127 degrees or something. I went to put my shoes on and my feet were burning, and I looked and my socks had worn through on the bottom. They were tucked around the toes. I had a black car, and I damned near burned my hand trying to open up the trunk so I could put the clubs in.

I went back to the room, swam some more, and at three o'clock, I went out to take a hike. I brought a little bottle of water, and when I got outside it was windy. It was like standing in front of steel mills, for crying out loud, burning up. I hiked up and down and all over and swam again.

I drove home to California, and the next day I had a physical and tests scheduled. My lungs are fine, my spleen, my kidneys, everything, and then they turn the monitor off and a cardiologist comes in. They flick a screen on and there's five big blotches on the picture and I'm like, "Oh, *shit*. What's that?" Those are blockages, I was told. I went and did the stress test and they said I flunked it. After that was all over I told the doctor what I did on the weekend.

The doctors said they had to do an angiogram, and they made me fill out papers that gave them permission to open me up if they found something. I had to come back the next day. Driving home I'm thinking about this, and I thought I was on *Candid Camera*. I said, "It's okay, boys, you've gone far enough now." I went home. I had no symptoms. The next morning I started packing some stuff. My wife said she thought I was just going in for a test. I said I had a bad, bad feeling. Something's up. I was preparing to be in there for surgery.

You're supposed to watch yourself when you're on the table. I remember getting prepped, and the next thing I know I have god-damned hoses all over me. They did a five-way bypass. I was shocked. Afterwards, I said, "What the hell happened?" The doctor said, "I think you were about three to five, maybe six months from a heart attack. You had one foot in the grave and one on a banana peel."

I said, "You're s----ing me." He said, "Nope, it would have been a massive one, and it would have been over."

I was very lucky.

***

Butkus avoided a heart attack because of the coincidental timing of his medical tests. He thought back to Chuck Hughes, who was running a pass pattern one minute and died on a football field the next without even taking a hit—without any type of a warning.

Because of his experience watching Hughes collapse and die on the field and his own no-warning surgery that probably saved his life, Butkus arranged for his own cardiologist to administer tests to the high school players in Pennsylvania involved with his reality TV show. The doctor flagged four of the teenagers as showing signs of something out of the ordinary.

"Nothing really serious," Butkus said. "But their parents were contacted and notified that somewhere down the line they should just pay attention to this."

Butkus had no damage to his system because he never had the heart attack. He just got some new pipes, as he put it. He was even planning a return to Death Valley for a little more hot-weather recreation.

"I can't run with my knee," Butkus said. "But I'll either ride a bike or do something there. It's kind of neat to go there when it's hot like that."

It's even better when you live to tell about it.

November 14, 1971

SOLDIER FIELD
CHICAGO BEARS 16 - WASHINGTON REDSKINS 15
By Dick Butkus

One reason the game was so memorable was because George Allen was coaching the Redskins, and back during the war with the American Football League, he was the guy who was supposed to keep me busy and keep me from going to the AFL. So I got to know George fairly well. We would have lunch every Friday. When he left the Bears as defensive coach and went to the Los Angeles Rams as head coach he tried to trade for me. He was going to trade all of his draft choices for me, but George Halas would never do it.

We played the Redskins late in the year, and they had to win some games to get into the playoffs. We tied the score with like a minute or two minutes left in the game. I was a blocking back when we scored. All we'd had to do was kick an extra point and hold them for a minute, and we win. Our quarterback, Bobby Douglass, was the holder for kicker Mac Percival, only the snap went over Douglass' head. Earlier in the game, I had been kicked or hit in the eye and my eye started swelling, so I couldn't see very well. I'm waiting for the kick, and I didn't hear nothing like cheering. I turned around, and I saw Douglass running around back there. Douglass picked the loose ball up and scrambled, going back to the 30- or 40-yard line.

I was the left up back, and I drifted into the end zone. He threw it to me for the exra point. My eye was shut and my depth perception was off, so when the ball came, I jumped and caught it around my waist. When I looked at the film, I went, "Oh, s—." I didn't have to jump. It was right there, you know? I couldn't see the ball. If I would have dropped that, oh man. Then we held them and beat George Allen and the Redskins. They won enough games to make the playoffs, anyway.

***

In the Bears' final statistics for the 1971 season, fans can find Butkus' name near the top of the interceptions list with four, at the top of the tackles list with 117, and at the bottom of the scoring list. That was before the NFL adopted the two-point coversion for runs or pass plays, so Butkus' catch went into the books as a single point—in need of a double asterisk explaining the throw from Douglass. All of those defensive guys always want to get in on the offense.

The pivotal play that made Butkus' other game of his life so memorable was not highlighted by frivolity. The key moment revolved around a tragedy, and what happened on the field that day returned almost as a flashback to Butkus years later when he confronted his own mortality.

2

HARLON HILL

The world Harlon Hill inhabited as a youngster had more in common with Huck Finn than George Halas. Pro football was almost as alien a sport as curling. In the small Alabama town where Hill grew up, of course, people did know the rules of the game, and they rooted with all of their hearts for the Crimson Tide. But in the days before cable TV, the Internet, and even national network television, pro football was more rumor than regular viewing diet in the rural south.

Hill, who was born on May 4, 1932, was a tremendous athlete at Lauderdale County High in Rogersville, Alabama, but unlike the high school stars of today, he did not aspire to become a professional. In fact, he said, he barely knew pro football existed and cheered for no particular team because he was exposed to no team.

There was no doubt that George Halas knew more about Harlon Hill than Hill knew about George Halas when they first had contact. Hill had stayed at home to play college football, attending Florence State Teachers College, where he was a four-year letterman and captain of the squad his junior and senior seasons.

More recently, the school has been known as North Alabama and had divine success at the small college level, winning several national championships. Even today, however, it's hard to make the claim that the school has ever produced a better football player than Hill. In the 1950s college football was not divided into so many divisions (I-A, II, III, NAIA) as it is today. There were big schools, and there were small schools. That's all.

In the 2000s, and for some time, football, baseball, and basketball have employed sophisticated scouting systems to ferret out talent in any small town, at any small college, in any out-of-the-way place. But half a century ago that was not true. A true diamond in the rough could be discovered and hidden exclusively by a traveling baseball scout. A football or basketball star might be spotted by one team and be unknown to another. It was easy for those who did not appear in newsreels, in big-city newspapers, or in major bowl games to be overlooked and bypassed. Halas himself relied on a network of former players and coaching friends to tip him off when a player of special ability materialized on the scene in unlikely quarters. They did not send videotape. They called him on the phone and talked up their find. Halas often made draft picks on their say-so.

Hill fit that description. Hill was such a fine college player, even at his off-the-main-highway school, that he was invited to compete in the Blue-Gray All-Star game at Christmas 1953. It helped that Hill was an Alabama fixture since the game was played in Montgomery.

Until that practice week Hill had never given the first thought to a career playing pro football. He intended to become a teacher and a coach. One of the Blue-Gray game assistant coaches passed on information about Hill to Halas, and Halas made his acquaintance with Hill through the telephone. It was not uncommon to draft players sight unseen, but there was always the chance another team would take a flyer on Hill, too, so being in the know was helpful.

Still, Halas must have been pretty sure that Hill's small-school background would keep him off the radar screens of other NFL teams because Papa Bear did not choose Hill until the 15th round of the 1954 draft—a draft that had 30 rounds. That was in the days when

Harlon Hill was a little-known wide receiver from little-known Florence State Teachers College in Alabama when Bears founder George Halas drafted him on a tip about the lanky player's abilities. Hill averaged a remarkable 25 yards per catch his rookie year.
© *Brace Photo*

NFL rosters only listed 33 players during the regular season. Spending a draft pick was less a vote of confidence in Hill than the offer of an opportunity to register at training camp.

There has never been a time when NFL teams selected a player so low expecting him to evolve into a marquee player. Heck, most of the time when teams selected at the lower numbers in the draft they were throwing darts. They were hoping for a gem, but counting on receiving nothing but a practice player who would be cut prior to the season. Sometimes they might draft kids as favors to certain coaches, or if they were sons of friends. With a 30-man draft there was little cost to earning a bit of goodwill. Stepping back from that charade, these days even with 53-man rosters, the NFL draft only lasts seven rounds. If a college player is not selected by then he is a free agent.

What set Hill apart from bottom-of-the-list draftees and made him a keeper were his physical attributes. At a time when receivers were not large, he stood 6 feet 3 inches, and weighed 199 pounds. He also had a sprinter's speed and a very long stride. It turned out that after Hill got his hands on a pass, he could run like a deer during shotgun season. He had the special capability of making cuts, staying on his feet, and gaining huge numbers of yards after the catch.

Not only did Hill defy the odds and make the Bears roster, he became a starter; and as a rookie he grabbed 45 passes for 1,124 yards and 12 touchdowns. His per-catch average was an astounding 25.0 yards a grab, still the Bears single-season record. Hill was chosen NFL rookie of the year that season and made All-Pro for the first of three straight seasons. In 1955, he was also the NFL's most valuable player. Hill, the man from the nowhere, small-town south, made Halas look like a genius.

Hill had no idea what to expect from training camp, in practice, or in game preparation. He just took what came, good, bad, or indifferent, and tried to fit into a new environment and produce. Hill was told that Halas didn't have much faith in rookies, but Halas started him right away. What made Hill successful was an ability to score lots of touchdowns at the highest level of the game.

Hill played with the Bears from 1954 through 1961. Then he spent three more years in the league with the Pittsburgh Steelers and Detroit Lions. For his career, he nabbed 233 passes, good for 40 touchdowns, and a first-rate per-catch average of 20.2.

Hill proved early on that he had a knack for putting six-pointers on the scoreboard, and he made his mark in the game of his life right away by winning a game with a 66-yard catch with 30 seconds remaining.

October 31, 1954

KEZAR STADIUM
CHICAGO BEARS 31 - SAN FRANCISCO 49ERS 27
By Harlon Hill

My rookie year I caught a career-high four touchdown passes against the San Francisco 49ers. It was my sixth game in the pros and we had already lost to San Franciso earlier in the season. I had started out playing a whole lot in the exhibition season, and I had a good first game against Detroit. It was the beginning of a good year.

I was not really intimidated by the new competition. Coach Halas didn't generally think rookies were ready to play. He had a different opinion of me, I reckon. Four-touchdown games don't come along very often.

I caught three touchdown passes from George Blanda and one from Ed Brown. I guess I caught one in every quarter. The last one was in the final seconds of the ball game.

When you're in a game like that, you don't think about the game, or what you're doing at what time. At the end, when you're trying to win the game, all you do is get in a hurry-up offense. When it's a close game and it's going back and forth, you just do your job. The Bears threw the long passes to me. They would throw short passes to Bill McColl and some others, but I usually had long passes. I was known for that in college, too.

I had some good years, but when I started slowing down, the Bears put me on defense, in the secondary, for a year. I got hurt, severely spraining my ankle. If that hadn't happened, I would have been good for two or three more years, I think.

***

Hill was only 30 when he retired in 1962. He said he probably enjoyed himself a little bit too much and could have worked harder. He lives in retirement in Killen, Alabama, only about eight miles from the school where he established his football reputation.

The extraordinary receiver, who had three seasons for the Bears where he averaged 23 yards per catch or more, still owns Chicago team records more than 40 years after he retired. Hill recorded 19 100-yard receiving games in his career.

Hill is still remembered as a phenomenon in small-college football. When he played for Florence State, it was a member of the NAIA. Although his statistics were not spectacular (except for his yards-per-catch totals) since the school used a run-oriented offense, Hill's all-around skills were appreciated.

In 1986, homage was paid to Hill's career when the trophy awarded each year to the best football player in NCAA Division II was named "The Harlon Hill Award." It is the Heisman Trophy of that division, and the administration of the award is handled in Florence. Hill had already been elected to the Helms Athletic Foundation Hall of Fame, received his undergraduate and masters degrees in education from North Alabama, and been inducted into that school's Athletic Hall of Fame. But it's hard to match having your name and career immortalized by a player-of-the-year award.

"It is an honor," Hill said. "I really didn't think much about it at first. But it's gone on to become a real status thing. Everybody else [in other divisions] had trophies for best players. People got to thinking about it, and they got to thinking about me. They asked me would I care if they used my name. They said the NCAA sanctioned it. I said to go ahead. It's grown into a real popular thing. It's well received."

Hill still follows his old pro team from afar—even when the Bears have endured those trying losing seasons that exasperate fans.

"I follow them," Hill said. "I get disgusted with them, but I follow them."

What Harlon Hill hasn't done lately is make a pilgrimage to Chicago to see the Bears in person.

"I haven't been in very good health for the last five years," Hill said. "But I've got a lot of good memories of Chicago. I'm going to try and go one more time."

3

RICK CASARES

Rick Casares was a tough-guy fullback, the type of player coming out of the backfield who might hit the big tacklers with his head and shoulder just as hard as they tried to hit him. He was a power back who had no fear, a featured ball carrier before fullbacks were turned into nearly full-time blockers.

"I had the most carries every year for five years for our team," Casares said. "These days would be less fun. I wouldn't be a fullback today or I wouldn't make it. Maybe I would be a tight end. I'd love to catch the ball in the secondary."

Ricardo Jose Casares was born July 4, 1931, in Tampa, Florida, and despite his adventures in Chicago, he is a Floridian through and through. Casares attended Thomas Jefferson High School in Tampa, then attended the University of Florida in Gainesville. After his retirement from football, Casares returned to the Sunshine State, and he lives in Tampa today.

As a high schooler in the same area, Casares frequented the local beaches.

"My boyhood was spent—like all of us here—on the beaches," Casares said. "Summer vacations we'd go to Clearwater. Clearwater Beach would be our destination every weekend. The [Gulf] Coast has got the best beaches, I think."

Casares was a star at Florida and made second team All-America his junior season. He was preparing for a great senior year send-off and was selected for several preseason All-America teams. The word was out on Casares, and he was sure to be a high NFL draft pick the next year. Only a funny thing happened—before he could play out his senior year, Casares was drafted by the U.S. Army instead.

There is no draft these days, and even in the 1970s when the war in Vietnam raged and a draft lottery was instituted, the United States did not interrupt college educations by plucking individuals off campuses and turning them into soldiers. Casares was two games into his senior season when the military call came. His selection came amidst a period of controversy when it was said that athletes were receiving preferential treatment.

"When I got drafted, it was astonishing," Casares said. "There really was a lot of pressure. I felt like I was Shanghaied, but it was the greatest thing that ever happened to me."

Casares could have been outraged, but examining his time in the service, he said the experience was a good tune-up for professional football.

"The Army really toughened me up," Casares said. "I got to play service ball, and we played against really fine teams at Quantico. When the Bears drafted me, they had to wait a year for me to get out of the Army. In the Army, I got bigger and faster and stronger. If I had gone straight through college to the pros, I don't know if I would have been as successful. I made all-service when I was in the Army."

Casares was 6 feet, 2 inches, and 226 pounds in his prime, and he was a second-round draft pick of the Bears in 1954. He did not suit up until 1955, though; and by then, he was a 24-year-old man, more hardened and full-grown than a just-finished-with-college kid. Given his military service, Casares was an atypical rookie. Still, he was not

As a fullback with speed, power, and toughness, Rick Casares was a star rusher and blocker in the 1950s, helping the Bears win the 1963 National Football League championship. © *Brace Photo*

sure how his coach, John "Paddy" Driscoll, and team owner George Halas pictured using him. Did he fit into the backfield? Or was he going to ride the pine?

That season the Bears lost their first three games. Casares was not an immediate starter. The fourth game on the schedule was against the Baltimore Colts for a second time, and Chicago was desperate for a win. Later in his career, Casares would start for the 1963 championship team, and he would rush for 190 yards in a game. But the game in which he was transformed from virtual unknown to key player provokes particularly warm feelings. The Bears got their win that day, and Casares jumpstarted his professional career in what he considers to be possibly the most meaningful pro game of his life.

October 16, 1955

WRIGLEY FIELD
CHICAGO BEARS 38 - BALTIMORE COLTS 10
By Rick Casares

Picking my favorite game is no contest—one sticks out to me during my rookie year. It's so dramatic that it defies belief, but every word of it is true.

I wasn't getting much playing time. I hadn't carried the ball much at all. That particular game, I got put into the lineup with halfback Bobby Watkins, another rookie, inside our 20-yard-line. I wasn't a starter. Halas just put me in, and not because of an injury to someone. We were calling safe plays. The first carry Bobby Watkins did a quick opener for about two yards. The next play Bobby got another three. We had a third down and about five yards to go near our 20-yard line.

Quarterback George Blanda called for another handoff to Watkins, but as we broke the huddle, Watkins said, "Rick, I got banged on the last play. I feel dizzy. Can you take this?" Our positions were pretty much interchangeable, and I knew his assignment. I hadn't carried the ball barely at all, so I said, "Sure." We were in a split formation, so we just switched, and I took over his spot. The play called was a "toss," a pitch back.

The ball was snapped, and Blanda was ready to toss the ball out. I could see in his eyes that he was surprised looking over at me and thinking, "What the hell is he doing there?" Fortunately, he went ahead and tossed it to me, and I went all of the way—81 yards—for a touchdown. The play started on the left, and then I cut back. I cut back a couple more times and wound up on the right side of the field.

I was in the clear all of the way, and then the Colts linebacker Bill Pellington came up and had a shot at me in the last 10 yards. I gave him a stiff-arm and dove into the end zone. It was the longest run from scrimmage in the NFL that year, and it made me the starting fullback. After that, they put the toss play in for the fullback, too.

That one play gave a push to my career. I had the best average per carry in the NFL (672 yards on 125 attempts for a 5.4 average). It was a big thing to establish myself. It was important for me to realize that I could take the toss and that I had the speed. So many people think of me as a bruising fullback, but every year I had a run for more than 50 yards for a touchdown. That was great for me—I worked on my speed and got faster.

Halas was a tough guy and a tough guy to impress, definitely as a rookie. He was a firebrand and a helluva competitor. He wasn't one to compliment you that much. I didn't realize until later when I saw the film that he did come over to me after that run and congratulate me. I didn't remember because a bunch of the guys were slapping me on the back when I came off the field. On the film, I saw that he came over, and he evidently said something like, "Nice going, kid."

Casares locked himself into the lineup for the next 10 years of his 12-year NFL career, before finishing up by playing with Washington and Miami for a year apiece. Casares' single most outstanding year statistically was 1956, when he rushed for 1,126 yards, caught 23 passes, and scored 14 touchdowns. The Bears also advanced to the NFL championship game to meet the Giants again—another memorable game in Casares' repertoire, even if it didn't produce the result the Bears wanted.

It was a game where history repeated itself, with the same two teams coping with an icy field much as they had in 1934 in what came to be called "The Sneaker Game". Casares scored the Bears' only touchdown on a nine-yard run when the score was 20-0.

December 30, 1956

YANKEE STADIUM
NEW YORK GIANTS 47 - CHICAGO BEARS 7
By Rick Casares

This was a sneaker game, too. The day before the championship game they made us practice on the sidelines at Yankee Stadium because the field was so soft they didn't want us to tear it up. The temperature was in the '50s and '60s. It was mild. That was at one o'clock in the afternoon. By four or five o'clock, the temperature started dropping, and it went down to 10 degrees or so. It froze the field solid that night, and the next day they took the tarp off that. We had on regular cleats, and when we came out to warm up, I was one of the first guys to fall on my face.

The field was frozen solid—just hard and slick. The story is that the Giants' defensive end, Andy Robustelli, owned a sporting goods store, and they had sneakers for the opening kickoff. They were ready. We kicked off to start the game, and the Giants brought the kickoff back 52 yards. Our guys were just sliding all over the place. It looked like they had on white tennis shoes. They had traction, and our guys were sliding by them. We changed our cleats, but the grip was, well ... we were barely able to manage it. We were favored by three points, and they ruined it.

The Giants often would win the east; and we would win the west a lot—but we didn't win it as often as we should have. In 1957, we were picked by everyone to win the world championship going away, but we made some changes and we finished next to last. In 1956 we had a great offensive team. I led the league in rushing, and Ed Brown led in passing. We scored 363 points in a 12-game season. We led the league in total offense, but the next year our offense changed a great deal. We tried to alternate quarterbacks, but that never works.

Zeke Bratkowski, a beautiful guy whom I love, came out of the Army and instead of using Ed Brown—who had led the league the year before, who was a great field general, and who had a lot to do with my success—Halas used Bratkowski. Ed Brown and I had our plays and our program, and the quarterback had the choice of what plays to call. I can count maybe five plays being sent in from the sideline at that time. We also had George Blanda, who was one of the greatest. We had Blanda; and we had Brown, but Halas liked Bratkowski. We were coming off the world championship and our reign only lasted one year. We could have won again.

The Bears were a mixed-up 5-7 in 1957, and Halas resumed coaching in 1958, steering the team to an 8-4 record. With Halas again on the sidelines, and the ascension of the Green Bay Packers under Vince Lombardi, the Bears-Packers rivalry intensified again.

"Whenever we played the Packers, it was the game of the year," Casares said. "Halas built that up. During his time, Halas instigated the preparation and intensity for the Packer game. We always played a good game against them. The feeling was there because they were located nearby and because the teams were such longtime rivals.

"Halas initiated the feeling from training camp on—not just the week of the games, no way. From the time we started practicing, even in the beginning of the year, the Packers would come up. We'd practice a particular play, and we would mothball it—say that we were going to save it for the Packer game. We would try it out, and if we liked it, then we would save it."

Some of the hardest fought games Casares played with the Bears were contests against the Packers and Baltimore, another very good team. A mutual respect existed between the top clubs, and the players got to know each other beyond the grunting and grabbing confrontations on the field when they lined up together at the Pro Bowl after the season.

"I got just as close to some of those guys as any I have in my whole career," Casares said. "The greatest defensive player I ever played against was Gino Marchetti, and the greatest offensively was Lenny Moore—both Colts. Lenny Moore was a game breaker, and Gino Marchetti was just awesome on defense."

Of course, Casares played with another of the greatest of defensive ends, Doug Atkins. Atkins was possibly the strongest player of the era, and he had no patience for offensive linemen who tried to hold him illegally if they couldn't stop him from getting to the quarterback legitimately.

"If somebody held Doug, he would kill whoever was in front of him," Casares said. "I saw him smacking and flipping over a 270-pound tackle, then knock over a back. They always double-teamed him, and he would get the quarterback unless somebody held him."

Once, Casares, Atkins, and some of the Colts were sitting around talking together at the Pro Bowl. As they relaxed, Lenny Moore innocently asked his Colts teammate, Jim Parker, widely regarded as one of the greatest offensive linemen of all time, "How come you don't hold Doug?" Parker said, "You think I'm crazy?"

"Doug was right there," Casares said, "and he just smiled. He was a wrecking crew. It was awesome the strength and athletic ability he had. Stan Jones, one of our linemen, was a great, great football player, and a great, great fellow. Stan was one of the first guys into weight training. He had a regimen with weights for his workouts, and the Bears were the only ones who did it then. But he wasn't as strong as Atkins."

As a young man coming out of the Army, Casares prepared to report to the Bears and meet with George Halas to sign a contract. He flew into Chicago the night before the rendezvous, and the way the town treated him before he ever donned a uniform solidified a lifetime's worth of good feelings in him.

"I loved it the day I got there," Casares said. "I met a cab driver who astonished me by looking in the mirror and saying, 'Aren't you Rick Casares?' It was my first time in Chicago. I said, 'That's my name.' I didn't know there had been anything in the paper about me, but they had published a picture and this guy remembered it and recognized me. And he said, 'We're happy to have you coming to the Bears.' I was astonished."

The evening did not end there. Casares asked the driver to take him to a good hotel, but the guy asked him if he liked music and said that he was going to a good club. Did Casares want to join him? Casares had the night free and only had a small carry bag because the plan was to stay just one night. He told the man he loved music and would be happy to go.

"So, he took me to the Blue Note," Casares said. "He took me in—he knew the owner and brought me with him. He brings me up to the guy and says, 'Look who I've got. Rick Casares of the Bears.' The owner said to sit down and have a drink. I'll never forget it. There was a great trombone player on that night, and I had the time of my life. That was my introduction to Chicago. I've loved it ever since."

A fit man in his 70s, Casares is still quite active, but he always makes time for an annual visit to Chicago to mingle with old teammates and talk with old Bears fans.

"It's one of the highlights of my life now, the response I get when I go back to Chicago," he said

Just a thank you for all of the highlights Rick Casares provided scoring touchdowns for the Bears.

4

MIKE DITKA

The big man stood in the entranceway of the restaurant between the bar and dining area, his colossal cigar preceding his body by what seemed like a baseball bat's length. He stopped, framed in the light, towering over the hostess and surveyed the bustling scene. It was all good.

The noise never ceased, but the whispers began. "Look." "It's him." "He's here tonight." The patrons were happy for a glimpse. The look on the man's face was severe, the same scowl that intimidated dozens of large men at once. When he smiled a moment later, the diners at the tables seemed to exhale.

"Iron" Mike Ditka, nicknamed appropriately for his powerful body and admirable will, was master of his domain on the football field. Now he is master of a very popular restaurant in Chicago that bears his name. Diners know that if their timing is right, as it was on this night, that they might be lucky enough to see the proprietor in the flesh, not merely in the many framed photographs and paintings adorning the walls.

Mike Ditka came out of Western Pennsylvania mining country as a fairly anonymous player to Bears fans. He evolved into one of the most popular players of his era, helping lead the team to the 1963 championship while revolutionizing the tight end position. Then he was anointed as head coach in one of Papa Bear George Halas' dying wishes. When, under his tutelage, the Bears of 1985 swept to a Super Bowl championship, the hard-nosed, explosive, demanding Ditka was elevated to sainthood. Now retired from coaching, a still-visible Ditka is on the "A" list of Chicago celebrities.

In Illinois, Ditka is better known than the governor and even had the chance a couple of years ago to inject himself into an Illinois U.S. Senate race. He chose not to represent the Republican ticket, but some people were salivating over what his stump speeches and debates promised. Ditka's opinion is sought after in all matters football; he raises money for charities through autograph and golfing events; records his thoughts in books; explains his viewpoints on football commentary shows; and is revered as a symbol of Chicago Bears successes of the past.

In many ways, the player and coach who always understood Chicago sensibilities without actually growing up in the city, is the embodiment of Da Bears. It might even be said that he is "Da Bear" himself. Humorously ironic, the signature meal on Ditka's restaurant menu is Da Pork Chop—what may well be the best pork chop served in America.

Hard to believe, Mike Ditka has permeated virtually all important moments in Bears history over the last 45 years—the good ones, anyway. During his presence, the Bears flourished. During his absence, the Bears declined. It is not a straight line of mathematical soundness, but something to consider. When Mike Ditka was on top of his game, so were the Bears.

Michael Keller Ditka was born October 18, 1939, in Aliquippa, Pennsylvania. An All-American at the University of Pittsburgh, he was the Bears' No. 1 draft choice in 1961.

"Most of my recognition in college came from playing defense," said Ditka, who excelled in the NFL as an All-Pro tight end. "We played both ways."

Young Mike Ditka, a Pro Football Hall of Famer as a tight end, sits on the bench next to his coach and mentor George Halas during Ditka's 1960s playing days. The duo won an NFL championship together in 1963. *Photo by Robert Riger/Getty Images*

From the moment Ditka joined the Bears, Halas recognized a kindred spirit who hungered for victory, was willing to put his body on the line, and was tough enough to mix nails with his raisin bran. For one who required unswerving devotion and believed in discipline as much as he believed in God, Ditka's streak of rebelliousness was his only problem. The same fiery disposition that helped Ditka wreak havoc on a field with 21 other combatants sometimes led him to contentious confrontations with the Old Man. And eventually Halas traded him away.

They were both strong personalities who believed in the same primary football truisms, but one was young and headstrong, and the other was a senior citizen unwilling to change his ways. Halas played a key role in developing Ditka as a pro, and even more critically, he innovatively found the proper position for him to play when there was little precedent.

What Halas did was turn the 6-foot-3, 228-pound Ditka into a pass-catching tight end. In the NFL today, tight ends are utilized as much for their good hands as their strength and blocking ability. However, in the early 1960s, tight ends were expected to be silent soliders. They were bonus linemen assigned to pick off rushing linebackers and to protect the quarterback. Once in a great while—in an emergency or a burst of magnanimity—the quarterback would throw a pass to the tight end to make him feel needed.

As a newcomer during the 1961 season, Ditka was the Bears' secret weapon. In a 14-game season, he caught 56 passes for 1,076 yards. Twelve of his catches went for touchdowns, and his per-catch average of 19.2 yards was phenomenal—especially for a player who was not a wide receiver. As a result, Ditka was selected the league's rookie of the year.

Although Ditka never again matched the touchdown total in a single year, his debut season set the tone for his career. Ditka played 12 seasons in the National Football League, the first six in Chicago.

He also played two years for the Philadelphia Eagles and four for the Dallas Cowboys. Ditka played on the Cowboys' 1971 Super Bowl-champion team that defeated the Miami Dolphins.

Ditka's stay in Dallas was significant for other reasons. He admired coach Tom Landry and learned from him. After retiring as a player Ditka joined the Dallas staff and received his initial coaching training with the Cowboys. What he absorbed there qualified him to become the head coach he became in Chicago.

In 1964, Ditka caught 75 passes, a record for tight ends that lasted until 1980, when the NFL schedule was expanded to 16 games. Ditka was chosen for the Pro Bowl after his first five seasons with the Bears.

During his career, Ditka caught 427 passes for 45 touchdowns and was selected for the Pro Football Hall of Fame in Canton, Ohio, in 1988. Ditka acknowledges that Halas' determination to transform him into a tight end who contributed heavily to the offense was a turning point in his career.

"I was really the first one," Ditka said. "I was the one they started throwing to. You've got to credit Halas with that. Until then, the tight end was just a tackle. I was the first one."

Ditka was a potent weapon on the Bears' 1963 championship team, and winning the title was his greatest thrill as a player. But his greatest individual game took place earlier that season, when he caught nine passes for 110 yards and four touchdowns in a single game.

October 13, 1963

LOS ANGELES COLISEUM
CHICAGO BEARS 52 - LOS ANGELES RAMS 14
By Mike Ditka

If you're talking about individual accomplishments, the game when I caught four touchdowns against the Rams was my best.

We were a better defensive team than offensive team that year. Only that game, we really crushed them. We never really scored that many points. We completed five touchdown passes against the Rams that day. I felt it was probably the greatest game I ever played in as a player, but it was a team effort. The 1963 championship game itself stands out more.

I was lucky I was even selected by the Bears in the draft. I didn't have an inkling at that time that Halas was going to make me a tight end—there were three other teams at the time who were very interested in me: the Pittsburgh Steelers, the Washington Redskins, and the San Francisco 49ers. If I was taken by any of them, I would have been a linebacker.

If I had been a linebacker in the NFL, my life would have been significantly different. I'm known because of what I did as a tight end. Hell, yeah, my life would have been different. I don't know if I would have been as good a linebacker.

The game against the Rams was one of those games where everything went right. Bill Wade kept throwing to me, and I kept running for touchdowns. Tight ends didn't score four touchdowns in a game. That was my greatest game, but the funny thing was that the best catch I ever made for the Bears came in a different game, and it was overshadowed.

It was in the game when Gale Sayers ran wild. I probably made the greatest catch I ever made. It was a one-handed catch, and I kept on going into the end zone. Nobody believed I caught it, but it seems insignificant because Sayers' effort was so phenomenal. My greatest catch and nobody remembers it.

***

In the years leading up to Halas' death in 1983, the Bears had slumped. Ditka was coaching in Dallas when he wrote a letter to his former boss explaining how he was a once-and-forever Bear who understood the organization and believed in the ideals of the franchise as exemplified by Halas. The letter sold the Old Man, and he hired Ditka to run the team. Irascible, frequently angry, often witty, regularly outspoken, rarely regarding players' feelings, Ditka coached the way he played—all out, all of the time. His short hair, mustache, and scowl were accessories to his explosive persona. Ditka said what he thought and meant what he said. He was photographed walking off the field in a dour mood and flashing his middle finger at the photographer.

He told his players that he was going to mold them into a championship team and provide the title for Halas, who had the faith to hire him. He bruised feelings and egos, and wore his passion on his sleeve. Chicago fans loved him because he shared and exhibited their want-to-win desire. His players cringed at his outbursts, but understood instinctively that he was willing to put himself on the line as nakedly and determinedly as they did to seek victory.

In 1985, a *Sports Illustrated* poll taken anonymously among NFL players revealed that many would not want to play for Ditka. He said he thought they must be stupid, and said Ditka the player would want to play for Ditka the coach "… because I want to win."

Win the Bears did. They finished the 1985 regular season 15-1 and then swept to the Super Bowl championship by crushing the New York Giants, the Los Angeles Rams, and the New England Patriots in the playoffs. The Bears devoured opponents with their defense— much as the 1963 team had. They scored more than enough to dominate, and they led the league in personality.

Ditka was a lightning rod for opposing fans who constantly baited him and were delighted when he swallowed the bait and shouted back. His defensive coordinator, Buddy Ryan, was blunt and tough, a fiery general whose troops loved him. Quarterback Jim McMahon clashed with authority, mooned a helicopter in New Orleans during the Super Bowl lead-up and was an inspirational leader for the offense. Defensive tackle William "The Refrigerator" Perry made America fall in love with him by bulling for a couple of short-yardage touchdowns on offense. And before the season culminated in the championship, several players contributed to the making of "The Super Bowl Shuffle" music video.

They were wild times in Chicago, and Ditka was the ringleader. It seemed he would lead the team forever. It didn't work out that way.

After 11 seasons at the helm, he was fired, and his farewell press conference in January 1993 was tearful. Ditka's lifetime Bears coaching record was 112-72, a .609 winning percentage. It's no wonder that such a mark on a resume combined with a Super Bowl title—the only one in team history—endures in fans' minds as some of their best of times.

One other reason Ditka's coaching regime was adored: he gave fresh life to the long-time rivalry with the Green Bay Packers, the most intense in franchise history and one that dates back to the beginnings of the NFL. The 1963 team Ditka played on interrupted the Packers' glory years under Vince Lombardi. The 1980s Bears teams Ditka coached at a time when Sixties Packer Forrest Gregg was leading Green Bay. The rivalry was never fiercer.

"When we played against Green Bay when I was playing, it was my opinion that we were playing against the best franchise I'd ever seen," Ditka said. "It was acknowledged that it was a knockdown, drag-out rivalry. We played our asses off. We respected the hell out of each other.

"Then we went through a period there, when I was coaching when we thought people were giving us cheap shots. Things kind of got out of hand. It never happened with Lombardi and Halas. It never happened with Bart Starr and me when he was coaching—only with Forrest Gregg. That's not the way football is meant to be played."

When the Bears were atop the football world, they were dominating and controversial, and they made the sport interesting. Fans couldn't wait to hear what Ditka said, and they couldn't wait to watch him blow his top. They laughed at the Fridge, were perplexed by McMahon, but were glad he was theirs. They were in awe of running back Walter Payton, whom Ditka called the best football player he ever saw. They had it good, and they knew it.

One thing about Ditka—he was never dull. You may not agree with him all of the time and you may wish he hadn't mouthed off. But it was all Ditka being Ditka, and where was the fun if he reined himself in and said, "No comment", or uttered a politically correct opinion? McMahon, who probably could have done with some public self-analysis himself, took to calling Ditka "Sybil" for his demonstrations of a split personality.

When Ditka was fired, McMahon, then playing for the Eagles, admitted that he and Ditka argued constantly, but "… we both wanted to win. I would've liked to have played with him. He's the kind of guy you'd want on your team. You always knew where you stood with the guy."

Ditka often said the perfect thing. When he summed up his Bears of the mid-1980s as a "bunch of Grabowskis," Chicagoans liked it. There was no way Mike Ditka was going to coach a team of prima donnas. That would be a bad fit. Ditka was not a guy given to vacillation and even said, "I don't condone everything I do." Above all, Ditka prized winning.

"I hate to lose," Ditka famously reported, and he said that feeling was born in him in Little League.

He always led as if it mattered. In November 1985, the Bears crushed Dallas, 44-0, for their first victory over the Cowboys in 14 years.

"It was awesome," Ditka said.

Ditka didn't want to gloat about topping his mentor, Landry, so he didn't say much more, but after the contest he gave game balls to every player on the team and promised to gold-plate one for backup quarterback Steve Fuller, who directed the offense. For a man who almost always wore his emotions on his sleeve, this time Ditka was verbally discreet, but his actions in passing out presents like that showed how much the win meant to him. That was Ditka.

After the Bears fired Ditka, he became a television football analyst. Then in a move that surprised some, he returned to the sidelines as a coach in 1997, trying to rebuild the New Orleans Saints. Although Ditka made close friends in the area while with the Saints, he never approached the success he had with the Bears.

Ditka was deeply touched by the terrible troubles suffered by New Orleans when Hurricane Katrina leveled the community. He recalled old friends and the ongoing woes of the cleanup and rebuilding disturbed him.

"You've got those things happening with the hurricane," Ditka said. "That will sober you up."

Ditka was sobered up when he endured a heart attack, but he still knows how to play to his old image on occasion. That may be why a recent book he co-authored with *Chicago Sun-Times* sports columnist Rick Telander was called *In Life, First You Kick Ass*. Clearly someone, the publisher, the co-author, the coach, believed that the willingness of the public to buy what Ditka had to say was rooted in his tried-and-true methods as coach.

The book is sub-titled "Reflections on the 1985 Bears and Wisdom from Da Coach." It appeared on shelves for the 20th anniversary of the Bears' wondrous Super Bowl achievement. Early in the book, Ditka wrote of the champs, "We had all kinds of people on that club, but they were focused like I was." That simple phrase might sum up why it all worked.

Despite revisiting those special times through the hindsight filter of two decades, the Ditka of today believes he is a different guy. Spending more of his time enjoying the success of his restaurant, being in demand for public engagements in and around Chicago, and watching football with an announcer's comparative detachment rather than a coach's intense involvement, Ditka suggested he has mellowed from the days he led the Bears to a championship as a player and to Super Bowl glory as a coach.

"I don't take myself too seriously anymore," Ditka said. "I've got my family. I've got my health. I try to enjoy my life. I don't get quite as aggravated as I used to. I try not to let things bother me as much. Well, maybe with golf I do."

His golf game bugs him. It's good to know that the growling Bear hasn't lost all of his bite.

5

STAN JONES

Stan Jones was a throwback to the 1930s style of football. During his career as a lineman with the Bears, Jones played guard and tackle on offense and defensive tackle on the other side of the ball. Not always in the same game. Sometimes he even alternated seasons. But in his Hall of Fame career he did go both ways, an increasing rarity after World War II as the game evolved and an age of specialization dawned.

Jones was a tough football player who sometimes looked tougher in photographs because his hair was cut extremely short and was tapered to a V in front. Jones stood 6 feet, 1 inch, and he played at right about 250 pounds. These days he would be a midget among the proliferation of 300-plus-pound linemen, but Jones began lifting weights to build up his strength long before weightlifting was popular among professional athletes. He said that gave him a useful advantage.

Born November 24, 1931, in Altoona, Pennsylvania, Jones played his high school ball in that football-rich state. He went to college at the University of Maryland and while there occasionally attended Washington Redskins games in the nearby District of Columbia. He never gave a thought to playing professional football at the time, however. Jones hoped to become an Air Force pilot, but he couldn't pass the physical. Genuine eyesight woes and football injuries have sidelined more military prospects over the years than those who imagined more exotic excuses. Rather than be drafted by the military, Jones was drafted by the Bears—in the fifth round in 1953.

Jones has few pleasant memories of his first training camp with the Bears. He makes it sound more like Army boot camp: a strict, barking coach, no air conditioning in the buildings. This was the time period when the Chicago club was training at St. Joseph's College in Indiana, and Jones hated it. He said the team employed a security guy—whom the players nicknamed Dick Tracy—whose sole job seemed to be to keep an eye on them and report rules infractions to management. Jones said the doors of the dorm were actually chained shut at night, something that definitely made it harder to evade bed checks and violate curfew. Not that Rensselaer, Indiana, offered much in the way of nightlife. Jones likes to use the word "penitentiary" when describing those summers.

However, after acclimating to the temporary monastery life, Jones went on to a Hall of Fame career. He played 13 seasons ending in 1966, all but one with the Bears. Jones was a key member of the 1963 team that won the National Football League title and whipped the New York Giants in the final game.

Jones then worked 27 seasons as an assistant coach in the NFL. He was elected to the Hall of Fame in 1991. Jones' off-season experiences illustrate how little money pro football players took home in the 1950s and early 1960s, especially when dealing with the frugal George Halas, the Bears' owner-coach and protector of the purse strings. Jones worked throughout the winter and spring as a school teacher in Maryland, and he now lives in retirement in Broomfield, Colorado, near his three grown children.

Jones coached for the Denver Broncos first, then the Buffalo Bills, and returned to Denver for the final 13 seasons of his pro coaching career. He was attracted to Colorado's beloved 14,000-foot peaks and

Hall of Fame lineman Stan Jones played offense and defense for the Bears at different times. He only weighed 250 pounds and jokes that he could never be a lineman in today's pro game. *Photo by AP/WWP*

the vast vistas they offered. When he was a little bit younger, Jones climbed those mountains, hiked all around the hills, and rode his bicycle in some of the high-altitude areas. After his wife died, Jones moved into an apartment to be closer to his children.

Jones first established himself in the NFL as a premier offensive lineman. He always dabbled in the role of defensive fill-in—a valuable versatility for a guy who spent much of his career on the Bears when the league only allowed 33-men rosters. But Jones went over to the other side full-time for the 1963 season, at a time when the rival Green Bay Packers ruled the roost under Vince Lombardi. When the season began, everyone thought the Packers—not the Bears—would be on top again come December.

The Bears, who finished 11-1-2 that year, opened the season with a game at Green Bay. It set the tone for the championship run—the Bears completed the title season with a 14-10 triumph over the Giants—and for Jones' switch to defense.

September 15, 1963

LAMBEAU FIELD
CHICAGO BEARS 10 - GREEN BAY PACKERS 3
By Stan Jones

The Bears moved two of us over to defense that year—me and Bob Kilcullen. We became the left side of the defensive line. George Allen took over the defense that year. I had decided to retire, and I didn't plan on playing that season; but George Allen asked me to come back and play defense. I kind of looked forward to that idea because it was different, so I said, "Yeah, I'll do it."

I had played defense before when there was an injury or something. My first two years of college I was strictly offense, and then in 1953, they got rid of the two-platoon system so you went both ways. Periodically, the Bears used me on defense on short-yardage plays. I was always in on short-yardage goal-line stands.

The year before, in 1962, I played a couple of games on defense because of injuries to other guys. But I had decided the heck with it, that it was time to hang them up. That's because it was so hard to keep moving my family to Chicago and back to Maryland. And we weren't making much money. Because I was teaching school I had a chance to become a high school coach and continue with my life's work. It was a temptation. It wouldn't make sense to quit today like that because of all the money the players make. I wasn't making much, and it took a lot to live in two places.

It was a big game because Green Bay was the world champion, and it was the opening game. Bill Gleason, the Chicago sportswriter, had written a column looking at the prospects of the Bears for the season, and he said we looked pretty solid on defense—except he had some questions about the left side of the line, with its two offensive guys and one of them a school teacher. That's me. I taught school in the off-season for 12 years.

I read the thing and thought, "Well, gee, it does look kind of bad." Here we were playing Green Bay, and we had the two new guys on the left side of the line. Anyway, the night before the game we were eating dinner at a place called The Spot in Green Bay, and Bill Gleason happened to be in there, too. Kilcullen saw him and said, "Hey, Bill, I just want you to know that Stan Jones and I are going to show up for that game no matter what you think." Or something like that. I said to Kilcullen, "Thanks a lot. What did you do that for?"

It didn't really bother me what Gleason had written. But sure enough as soon as the game began, the Packers ran right at me and Bob. Jim Taylor, the tough fullback, was doing most of the running. We were playing against the usual group on the Packers' line—Forrest Gregg and Jerry Kramer. They came after us pretty good. We didn't have to go chasing around looking for them because they came right at us, and, my God, we went out and beat them.

It was a 10-3 game. We didn't allow them to score a touchdown. It was a great moment. I want to tell you the satisfaction of that win was huge. On the train on the way home, we celebrated a little bit.

The next day Gleason wrote a poem in honor of Kilcullen and me, and put it in his column. I don't have it now, but it was very satisfying to read.

***

For years, Jones had enjoyed himself competing in the most anonymous of positions—guard and tackle—content to open holes for the running backs and act as guardian of his quarterback.

"I liked it because I was doing fairly well at it," Jones said. "I liked the idea of doing the work because we had some good runners behind us. Our fullback, Rick Casares, had 1,000 yards, so it was rewarding. I didn't like defense as well. But then in 1963, I was playing on a defense that set all kinds of records. We only gave up 144 points. It was a defense that had good people on it—Bill George and Doug Atkins and Richie Petitbon."

Many things were different in the NFL during Jones' heyday. Salaries were low, and responsibilities were high. Not only could a star offensive lineman occasionally get pressed into duty on defense, he became a regular on special teams, blocking on kickoffs.

The Bears of the 1950s and 1960s were a paternalistic outfit. George Halas was Papa Bear in more ways than one. Jones said Halas at various times came off more as a businessman than football coach. Typically, Halas seemed as generous as the IRS.

"He was hard on the outside, of course," Jones said. "He was always afraid somebody was going to ask for money."

Most players who stayed with the team very long, however, gradually sensed that despite Halas' outer gruffness, he cared about them. When a player suffered a hardship or a tragedy, Halas would ante up cash to cover their needs almost as if he had a secret slush fund to be tapped only in case of emergency.

Sometimes, at unexpected times, Halas also dispensed sentiment, letting a player show how he really felt even long after he had become an ex-Bear. Jones experienced this while an assistant coach with the Broncos. One Christmas week, Jones was at the Blue-Gray college all-star game in Montgomery, Alabama, scouting the senior players for the upcoming NFL draft. The phone rang in Jones' hotel room, and he was surprised to hear the voice of then-Bears assistant coach Jim Dooley, a former end whose Chicago playing tenure overlapped heavily with Jones'.

"Dooley called and said, 'How you doing?'" Jones said. "And 'Blah, blah, blah, how do you like the job,' and he kept on going. Finally, I said, 'Hey, Jim, I know you're really interested in my welfare here, but this is a little bit unusual. What is this all about?'

"And he said, 'Well, to be honest with you, Halas asked me to call you to see how you were doing. He wanted me to tell you that you're never going to be less than part of the family here.'"

The call was a surprise. Jones told Dooley it was a nice thing to do, admitting he was touched by the gesture.

"That's the kind of thing Halas did," Jones said. "He showed he had that feeling for us deep down."

The 1963 team provided Halas with his last championship—the only title team Jones played on, though he had participated in the 47-7 title game loss to the Giants in 1956. Living with that disappointing defeat made the turnaround result seven years later even sweeter.

"It was always nice to beat the Giants," Jones said. "It was a big thing."

And to walk off the field knowing you were a world champion made it even bigger.

6

DOUG ATKINS

Big Doug Atkins was a quarterback killer at defensive end. Many believe Atkins was the strongest man in pro football during the 17 years he played between 1953 and 1969, a Hercules on the gridiron, a Hulk in orange and blue rather than green skin. Atkins started in the pros with the Cleveland Browns, who made him a No. 1 draft pick, spent 12 seasons with the Bears, and finished up his last three seasons with the expansion New Orleans Saints.

Hall of Famer Weeb Ewbank, who coached the Baltimore Colts and New York Jets to NFL championships, described Atkins as "... the most magnificent physical specimen I had ever seen."

Atkins stood 6 feet, 8 inches, and weighed 275 pounds during an era when linemen were typically 30 or more pounds lighter. That's one thing that made Atkins hard to block. Another was his ornery, get-the-quarterback mind-set that paid very handsome dividends when he crashed into the opposition's backfield.

The big guy's power made him a handful for offensive linemen, but that was not Atkins' only attribute. He was a terrific all-around athlete and showed it at the University of Tennessee. Atkins first came to the Vols' attention as a basketball player and enrolled on scholarship in Knoxville. Once on campus, he also took up track and field and won the Southeastern Conference high jump title. Atkins attacked the role of defensive end with the spirit, fury, and possessiveness of King Kong—a man bigger than most foes, and harder to handle. He could not abide being held or tripped, and if any lineman was foolish enough to try to stop him illegally, an infuriated Atkins likely just tossed him aside and munched the quarterback for lunch. Atkins' temper was one personality trait that made him so feared on the field.

The late Johnny Unitas of the Baltimore Colts once said, "One of his favorite tricks was to throw a blocker at the quarterback."

Now that's strong—just pick up the blocker and heave him.

Atkins also was a fun-loving guy and had little tolerance for any type of administrative restrictiveness. He played the game with abandon, but did not wish to be subjected to many rules off the field. For that reason, he often proved irksome to Bears leader George Halas who preferred everyone to conform. In one famous story, Halas, attempted to administer punishment to Atkins for an infraction, yelling, "Take a lap—and wear your helmet!" Except for wearing his helmet as instructed, Atkins appeared for his run in the nude. The consistent insubordination, as Halas saw it, likely led to Atkins being transferred to New Orleans.

The great end Tom Fears, said, "They threw away the mold when they made Doug. There will never be another like him." It wasn't clear if Fears meant on the field or off; or perhaps he was combining Atkins' uniqueness into a single, neat summary.

Doug Atkins was born May 8, 1930, in Humboldt, Tennessee, and still resides in the state. During his playing career, Atkins competed in eight pro bowls—all when he was with the Bears—and when he retired in 1969, his total of 205 games played set the record for a defensive lineman.

Atkins, who was elected to the Pro Football Hall of Fame in 1982, was a member of the Bears' vaunted defense that helped bring the 1963 world championship to Chicago.

The big tackle is not very sentimental. If there is one game that stands out at all in his memory, Atkins cites the 1963 title game

When Doug Atkins played in the 1950s and 1960s, pro linemen were considered large if they weighed 250 pounds. Atkins was a mountain of a man (6 feet, 8 inches, and 280 pounds), and many considered him the strongest player of his era. © *Brace Photo*

victory over New York, but what he truly remembers best is the friendships formed with teammates and the camaraderie of being Bears and making sense out of playing under an aging George Halas.

An anthology of history was a backdrop when the Bears met the Giants for the title. The Bears and Giants had met five times for the world title prior to 1963, and the Giants had reached the league's title game in five of the six previous years.

The weather was cold, with temperatures dropping to eight degrees at Wrigley Field, although the sun was out. Twice burned by the Giants in championship games during which the New Yorkers wore sneakers for better gripping than cleats, Halas was determined that his home field would be protected before the game and would not freeze. The ice was not a decisive factor this time, but as soon as the tarpulin came off, the cold did freeze the field and turn it slicker than an Ice Capades rink. This was a disappointment to those who thought Halas was God. It was proof he could not control the weather.

December 29, 1963

WRIGLEY FIELD
CHICAGO BEARS 14 - NEW YORK GIANTS 10
By Doug Atkins

To most of us, it seemed just like a regular game day. Playing in a championship game itself compared to a regular game, it's not too different. You're still playing a ball game, whether it's got a title attached to it or not. You just play the same way. You can't change anything that you've been doing all year, the rest of the year, with your offense and defense.

We didn't have too many cheerleaders out there trying to get us excited about it. We kept the emotion inside. You don't want to shout too much or think about too much, or count out the opposition. If you make a comment and somebody else magnifies it a little bit, then it riles them up.

We were known more for our defense, and the Giants more for their offense. We honestly didn't know if we were the best team. We didn't know what they were all about. They had an awfully good offense, and ours was good enough to win; but it seemed like they were supposed to be pretty strong. That worried everybody. We didn't know if we could hold them or not. We got a little luck early in the game. One of our linebackers, Larry Morris, intercepted a pass and ran it almost all of the way back. I think that pass helped us an awful lot.

We were known for our defense, but our offense was better than most people thought we had. We didn't make any mistakes, didn't have any turnovers. We scored when we got the opportunity. Many people called us "The Monsters of the Midway," bringing back the old nickname. But I never paid any attention to it. We were no bigger than the teams we played, maybe even smaller. I always thought the nickname was one of Halas' gimmicks.

Halas was good in his day. When football changed, Coach Halas didn't change too much. He kept the same old people around the team. But he knew his football. When people are changing things, if you don't change with them, it kind of hurts you a little bit. He kept the same old people around him, all the coaches, whether they did a bad job or a good job, it didn't make any difference. Instead of giving the old folks a raise, he would give them a title. That was all they wanted. They worshipped Mr. Halas.

You never knew what Halas liked. He'd never tell you what he liked. He kept that to himself. He always thought carefully about everything he said, wanting to know everything that was happening. We just did what we were told to do, and that was all we could do.

He didn't compliment us too often. He always wanted something more out of you. He always wanted more and more. He was a different man. It was a different time when he started out than when I played, so it's difficult to compare. He was one of the last old-timers to hang on when football was changing. Most of the rest of them were gone. You have to read the books to understand how he had things in the old days, running the team, running the league almost. Things were tough financially. They were just hanging on, so in his mind, he could pay a coach pretty much the same way he always did and the players.

He did everything that made Chicago known, and he had as much power in Chicago at one time as anyone, and I guess it was because he knew everyone.

Going into the championship game, Halas stressed that you keep your mouth shut until it's over with and not talk too much about what was going to happen. When the game ended and we won, we busted loose, and we enjoyed it. Everybody was happy. It didn't matter much that it was the Giants, even though the teams played so often. It could have been anybody. We were champions. I can't say that winning the championship game was the best thing that ever happened. I just say it was wonderful to win it.

***

Atkins was long past the rah-rah stage in his football career by 1963. He said that was for high school and college players, but as a pro, you knew you were laboring at a profession.

"Some games you felt you did a little better than in others, but to me it was just a job," Atkins said. "All the glory in college and high school was in the past. It was just a way to make a living. I never did any 'hooray' when we won a game and they lost a game. I never did feel that."

Although teammates from the 1960s era and other pros concede Atkins the strongest-man-in-the-league title, he does not make a similar boast himself.

"I don't know," he said. "I was pretty strong, but I guess every team had their strongest man. We never did match up with anyone. I wasn't much of an arm wrestler, anyway. With longer arms, I might have been better. I wasn't much of a weight man, either, you know? I guess you'd call it 'natural strength.'"

One player who seemed to have the best success matching brawn with Atkins was the late Baltimore Colts lineman Jim Parker, a Hall of Famer whom many defenders of the era call their toughest opponent to get past.

"Jim Parker is the one who stands out in my mind," Atkins said of the 6-foot-3, 273-pound Ohio State alumnus who played between 1957 and 1967. "I had a lot of problems with several guys. The ones who weren't supposed to be good ball players sometimes played a better game against you than the ones who were supposed to be good. But Jim Parker always stood out—you didn't have an easy game against him. He was the best as far as I'm concerned. At tackle, he was a lot better than the others."

Parker, who was all-league eight times, was forced into an early retirement by a knee injury, but was elected to the Hall of Fame in 1973. Reminiscing about the early days of his career, however, Parker once described his rookie season encounter with Atkins, of whom he said might have driven him prematurely from football.

"I played against some mean ones, but I never met anyone meaner than Atkins," Parker said. "After my first meeting with him, I really wanted to quit pro football. He just beat the hell out of me. It was awful."

Parker said his coaches boosted his morale with a pep talk, letting him know he would not see Atkins like every Sunday.

It is sad and somewhat ironic that Atkins, who had phenomenal mobility as a young athlete, is now hindered in his movements. Atkins has not returned to Chicago for a visit in years and mostly spends his time in the Knoxville area because of the lingering effects of a non-football injury suffered doing the simplest thing—sitting down.

About five years ago, Atkins was appearing at a sports memorabilia show in Canton, Ohio, site of the Football Hall of Fame, to sign autographs.

"I had a little problem," Atkins said. "I was sitting down, and I couldn't get up. I had a cracked hip."

He went into the hospital for surgery, but it didn't fix the problem the way he expected.

"I never did get right after I got out of the hospital," Atkins said. "I'd have liked to die. They worked my legs in rehab, and it helped with what little I've been walking. I've had a tough time. I'm kind of laid up here in Tennessee."

Atkins is sometimes cynical about the limited pension that older NFL players receive as well. This is a problem in other professional sports, such as the NBA, too. When the public considers the circumstances of modern pro athletes they are all lumped together as millionaires who have everything they want in life, from bling-bling to Ferraris. Players of earlier generations did not make the big bucks, however, and that is one reason they are out signing autographs for cash on the memorabilia circuit. That income supplements smaller pensions and may be needed very much.

"They sure are making a lot of money from those TV contracts," Atkins said of pro football executives. "But they're not passing any of it down to old players that played and helped build the league and whose bodies are busted up. You're crippled up, and you can't do anything, but they sure don't give you much of anything."

Although the ex-players do not rendezvous in Chicago, the relationships forged during his Bears playing days live on via long distance. Atkins talks on the phone to several of the old boys like offensive lineman Stan Jones, defensive lineman Bob Kilcullen, quarterback Bill Wade, and linebacker Joe Fortunato.

"There are several players I talk to," Atkins said. "Sometimes I talk to several people from other teams, too, when I feel like it. We get together on the phone and talk about the old things."

Atkins recalls good laughs and retains good memories from hanging out with the guys at Wrigley Field, too. He remembers one time a Coca-Cola had been left idle and a player coming into the clubhouse after a game guzzled a couple of swallows. He abruptly spit it out because it tasted so bad.

"I think Halas had a little toddy at halftime and put it in the Coca-Cola can," Atkins said. "We had some characters. It was a lot of fun playing there. There was a lot of fun going on."

It was always serious business when the Bears played the Green Bay Packers, though. Almost too serious. In the 1950s, the Packers were down. They fielded some of the worst teams in the league, but then at the end of the decade, the team's savior, Vince Lombardi, arrived. He revamped the squad, gathered talent, and instilled pride. And suddenly, just as they had been over many years in the past, the Packers emerged as a formidable Bears rival once again.

"To me it was just another game," Atkins said of the rivalry. "But I'd rather not play them at all when they were good. I'd rather play a weaker team. We got stuck with them twice a year, and we'd make the best of it. I remember all of them were pretty tough. If you played against Lombardi, you knew you were going to play a tough game."

During the 1963 championship run the Bears really did make the best of it, defeating Green Bay 10-3 and 26-7 in the regular season.

One thing that astonishes Atkins these days is the number of times he sees on television or reads in the newspaper about an NFL player being arrested for some particularly dastardly sort of mayhem. The cases range from murder to rape, to drug dealing, and players are not only getting suspended, but arrested and going to jail. It bothers him that the sport he loves is being sullied.

"Sometimes it seems as if you have a bunch of criminals playing the game," he said. "I hate to say it. There's some good people, but it's a shame they let the game get out of hand like they did. They thought our character was bad because we drank a little beer. They're into everything now. You name it. I guarantee you, if some of the old, old football people were still there, it wouldn't happen. It's a good thing they're cracking down on drugs, because the Nationall Football League is as bad as any of them. We had a bunch of good people. We didn't have any gangsters on the team or any people who do what these people do today."

Atkins was one of the great players of his time and was a popular player with the Bears. He cherishes his time spent in Chicago and is pleased to hear that he is favorably remembered in a city that loves its Bears heroes. Atkins said he thinks old-timers have the advantage over current players in being remembered fondly because they mingled more, came off more as regular guys. They weren't rich recluses.

"We mixed with people more than the players now," Atkins said. "Some people go around in limousines and things. We were more of the average person's team back then. Now they're a team of big shots. They got all of this money, and they don't know what to do with it. It was a little different when I played. Old-timers go away real quick, though. It's your stars that people remember best, and all of the people who used to be your fans, they're already dead.

"Not so many people go for the linemen. And the ones who were your age, well they only live so long and then they're gone, so there's nobody left to support you now. Oh, I guess there are a few of them old-timers still around Chicago. I settled in different places when I played, and I got along with all of the fans. That's good if they still remember me as a player. I liked Chicago. I enjoyed Chicago."

And although it doesn't always sound like it from the way he talks, Atkins did enjoy playing the game. What were his favorite things?

"Pay day," Atkins said laughing. "And when you won."

Those were the spoils of a job that is also a sport.

7

RICHIE PETITBON

The French-sounding last name made perfect sense for someone from New Orleans, where the beignets made the sweet tooth water and the shellfish were usually prepared with some kick. Born April 18, 1938, Rich Petitbon grew up in the jazz city and played college football at Tulane.

Especially for the time, he was a good-sized defensive back at 6 feet, 3 inches, and 206 pounds, and he sniffed the ball out of the air the way tourists nosed around for the snazziest restaurants in his hometown. Petitbon was a fleet runner and sure tackler. In a pro football career that began in 1959 with the Chicago Bears as a second-round draft pick and concluded in 1972 with the Washington Redskins (with a stop on the Los Angeles Rams' roster in between), Petitbon intercepted 48 passes. He led the Bears in that category three seasons.

In 1962, his six steals were good for 212 return yards, a total that led the league. There was good reason for the big return yardage. One of Petitbon's interceptions was run back 101 yards for a still-standing team record. Even in his second-to-last playing season, when Petitbon was 33, he intercepted five passes for Washington.

Some secondary players excel at man-to-man coverage. Some make their mark in zone defense. Some players gain such a fearsome reputation of being impossible to throw against that their statistics feature a bunch of zeros. Quarterbacks are too timid to aim passes in their direction. Petitbon's talent, far and away, was his ability to grab passes unintended for his use. His thefts changed the makeup and content of games, giving his teams offensive opportunities, while preventing the opposition from acting out their favorite offensive fantasies.

Petitbon was a stopper in every sense of the word—not a behemoth in the line who smashed blockers and rearranged fading quarterbacks' bone structures, not a linebacker who came from nowhere to destroy a play. Mostly, Petitbon demoralized enemy teams by simultaneously crushing their spirits and their drives downfield. Nearly 40 years after leaving the Bears' lineup, Petitbon still ranked third on the squad's all-time list of leaders in takeaways. He intercepted 37 passes and recovered seven fumbles while in a Bears uniform.

For most of his playing career, Petitbon roamed the defensive backfield for the Bears. He stayed in Chicago until 1968 before putting in two seasons in Los Angeles and two more in Washington. The shift to Washington turned into a life-changing team switch. When he retired, Petitbon moved into coaching. Most of his time spent as an NFL assistant, from 1978 to 1992, was on the Redskins' sideline. In 1993, Petitbon spent a single, somewhat disappointing season as Washington's head coach. The team finished 4-12.

When he retired from coaching he remained in the D.C. area and still lives in Virginia, where he now spends more time playing golf than watching football. One reason he settled in Virginia rather than returning to Chicago was the warmer weather. Petitbon doesn't miss winter or the harsh winds blowing off Lake Michigan.

Interestingly, Petitbon saved little in the way of memorabilia or photographs from his NFL days, though he does have some pictures adorning his house.

Defensive back Rich Petitbon had a knack for intercepting passes with the Bears and later had a long NFL coaching career with the Washington Redskins. *Photo by AP/WWP*

"I really didn't keep much," Petitbon said. "Most of the stuff that I have is framed."

Petitbon played and coached a long time in the National Football League. He outlasted most of his teammates and contemporaries on the field. But he has no hesitation in selecting the most memorable game he was part of—the 1963 Bears title-winning contest.

On that day, the Giants scored first on a 14-yard pass from Y.A. Tittle, the future Hall of Fame quarterback, to Frank Gifford. Don Chandler kicked the extra point. The Bears retaliated on quarterback Bill Wade's two-yard run followed by the extra-point boot by Bob Jencks to complete the first-quarter scoring.

Chandler kicked a 13-yard field goal in the second quarter for a 10-7 New York lead at the half. Then Wade's one-yard run and Jencks' kick gave the Bears the lead back in the third quarter. There was no more scoring in the contest that Pettibon remembers fondly and above all others.

The Bears' renowned defense—which registered 51 takeaways in a 14-game regular season—intercepted five passes that day to provide coach George Halas the last championship of his lengthy NFL career.

December 29, 1963

WRIGLEY FIELD
CHICAGO BEARS 14 - NEW YORK GIANTS 10
By Rich Petitbon

You know there are so few championship games that you ever play in, if you're lucky. It was a good game. We won, and I intercepted a pass on the last play of the game. It sure was a close one.

Going into the game, the town was hungry for a Bears championship. Chicago has always been a Bears town. The White Sox never seemed to catch on, and they've had many teams better than the Cubs. But it was always the Bears more than the Cubs. The Bulls kind of caught fire with Michael Jordan, but the Bears always seemed to capture the heart of Chicago.

The championship day was cold. The temperature was in single digits. I've heard various things, but it had to be five degrees. The field was frozen, and it was cold, cold, cold. I don't know how we played. I really mean it. I don't think the weather overall is as cold now as it used to be. When I watch games I don't see these frozen fields and the ice storms and the stuff that we played in. I think things have changed. Maybe it's that global warming. I think the seasons are changing, that the winters are not as cold.

But that day was cold.

I'll tell you how cold it was: they had these portable heaters for us on the sidelines that they put in temporarily. When you came off the field you could go by the heaters, and they would blow hot air onto you. You might just stick your foot by the heater to kind of warm it up a little bit. At one point, Joe Fortunato, one of our linebackers, had his foot by the heater, and I looked down and yelled, "Joe! Your damned shoe is on fire!" That's how cold it was. He didn't even feel the heat. He could have burned his foot up. Man, it was something.

We didn't even wear gloves on our hands—back then they didn't have appropriate gloves. If you wore gloves, you didn't think you could get a good grip on the ball if it came your way. And if you wore gloves, your teammates and the other team would think you would be showing weakness. To tell you the truth, I don't think I would have worn gloves anyway. My history with gloves in general was that once the glove got frozen, your hands were sort of dead. Even back then, they did have those little hand warmers, those things you can put in your pocket and warm your hands up once you get going. Some people didn't think they were even invented in 1963, but we had them.

The one thing we had going for us that you couldn't measure, of course, was adrenaline. On the day of a championship game, you were going to be really psyched up to play. Once your adrenaline gets going, you really don't feel the cold, except when you're on the sidelines. I felt sorry for the guys who didn't play—for a punter or a guy who just went in to kick field goals, having to stand around for most of the game. But playing, once your body got going, you didn't really feel it that much.

It was a big day. We had a great defense. It was a dominating defense that year. The Giants had a great offense with Y.A. Tittle at quarterback. I think he threw 36 touchdown passes that year. He threw to Del Shofner a lot. But Doug Atkins, our big, strong defensive end, put Tittle out of the game. He ran him over like a train. In those days, the defensive players could still hit quarterbacks. It's a little different game today. You can't touch the quarterback without being penalized anymore.

Shofner was Tittle's favorite receiver, and Tittle also liked to throw to Frank Gifford, the guy who was the announcer on *Monday Night Football*. Gifford was a good athlete, but he was a little over-rated. The Giants really did have a good offensive football team. It was their offense against our defense. Playing in the cold and keeping the score down was what we had to do to win, and playing at home helped us.

The game was close the whole way, and, although we had the lead, we didn't really have control of it. The Giants put Tittle back in the game. He probably shouldn't have been playing. I think he had a concussion. He really wasn't in top form, he really couldn't throw to the best of his ability. But I suppose it made sense in the end when you're going for a championship to put your best guy out there.

The clock was ticking down, and the Giants were moving down the field. They still had time to score a touchdown and win. Finally, they got pretty close to the end zone, and Tittle faded back and threw to Shofner. It nearly came right to me. It was a wobbly duck of a pass, and all I had to do was catch the ball. When I caught it, that was the game—there were only about 14 seconds left on the clock.

And do you know what my first thoughts were? "I don't want this to end."

That's a strange feeling, because most of the time it's a sigh of relief in a situation like that. I was glad we had it won, but the excitement was so great, I didn't want the game to be over. Sure, I felt some relief, and winning the championship is a great feeling. I just wanted to keep playing football.

***

Winning a title trumps all other good playing memories that Petitbon carries with him from the Bears, including once intercepting three passes off Bart Starr in a Green Bay Packers game. As always, the Packers-Bears rivalry created big-time seismic conditions in Chicago's mood based on victory or defeat.

"It was intense," Petitbon said. "The games were closer then. It seems that in more recent years the Packers dominate or the Bears dominate. It hasn't been a deal where you play two games and you split them all the time. It was really exciting when we played. Brett Favre has set it apart for Green Bay recently. And when the Bears had Jim McMahon, the Packers had nobody. So it's probably a quarterback deal."

Petitbon had the good fortune to spend many years in Washington, too, another fanatical football town. For decades, the Redskins were the farthest south community in the NFL, and their games were televised all down the Eastern seaboard. There is still a residue of Redskins mania in North Carolina, South Carolina, Virginia, Tennessee, and even Georgia, though the Falcons have supplanted much of the southern base.

"The Redskins do have their loyal fans," Petitbon said. "There's no question about that."

In some ways, Petitbon follows his old Bears teammates from afar. He knew that some ex-players were involved with broadcast work, and he was aware that Da Coach, Mike Ditka, who played with Petitbon, had recently led the singing of "Take Me Out to the Ballgame" during the seventh-inning stretch at a Cubs game.

"Terrible," Petitbon said of Ditka's singing voice. "Terrible, terrible rendition."

Once Ditka gets wind of that review, no telling what he'll tell Petitbon at their next Bears reunion. Petitbon, who does not often venture to Chicago, did return in 2003 for a 40th-anniversary gathering of the 1963 title team.

"That was a special deal to celebrate the 1963 team. I got to see all of the guys then," Petitbon said. "It was nice. It was amazing, though, to see those guys and think, 'Oh man, everybody looks so old.'

"And then I'm saying to myself, 'You ought to look in the mirror, you jerk.'"

8

J.C. CAROLINE

Members of the Bears between 1956 and 1965 couldn't tell whether their get-well cards from J.C. Caroline were heartfelt or not. Perhaps that's because Caroline was used to playing both ways as a human get-well replacement for the Bears on offense or defense—just rarely at the same time.

Although he was born James C. Caroline, his name was shortened to initials during his sports career. In fact, Bears fans remember him only by his initials and would have little clue who one was talking about if Caroline was referred to by his Christian name.

J.C. Caroline was born January 17, 1933, in Warrenton, Georgia, attended high school in Columbia, South Carolina, but went to college at the University of Illinois. A track star before he became a football player, in 1953, Caroline rushed for 1,256 yards, breaking Red Grange's single-season school record.

After spending a year in the Canadian Football League with the Montreal Alouettes, he joined the Bears as a 1956 seventh-round draft pick. Caroline played the season in Canada because he was ineligible for the Fighting Illini. However, he later finished his degree at Florida A&M in 1967 and returned to work as an assistant coach at Illinois into the mid-1970s.

A review of Caroline's NFL career statistics makes for fascinating reading. Some years, he played exclusively on defense. Some years, he got chances to run the ball. He also occasionally caught a pass, and some years, he was the Bears' primary kickoff return man, while also delivering big special-teams hits. He was the Bears' utility infielder. Caroline did a little bit of everything, most of it well, and made himself too valuable to be overlooked whenever a hole needed filling. Caroline brought speed to the lineup, which convinced coaches to deploy him in various roles.

The Bears made the most use of Caroline going both ways during his rookie year, when he rushed for 141 yards but also intercepted a career-high six passes. During the championship season of 1963, Caroline played solely on defense.

"Usually, if a guy was on offense and someone got hurt, I would play a couple of games both ways, and as soon as the other guy got his health back, I would go back to offense," Caroline said. "It didn't bother me none. I played both ways in college."

After retirement from football, Caroline returned to the University of Illinois area, taught physical education to junior high students, and taught driver's education at Urbana High School. He was also head coach of the football team there for five years. Caroline closely follows the adventures of his alma mater on the football field and on the basketball court—and was especially enthralled at the basketball team's run to the 2005 national championship game before losing to North Carolina for the NCAA title.

Caroline singles out few favorite games from his pro career, but revels in discussing the overall experience of playing for the Bears, playing both offense and defense, and how the sport treated him and has changed.

"One thing I can tell you about how the game of professional football has changed since I was playing is that overall the guys are bigger," Caroline said. "I am six feet tall, and I played at 185 pounds.

If a Bear got hurt on offense *or* defense, coach George Halas usually turned to the same man—J.C. Caroline—to fill the hole. The versatile Caroline didn't care which side of the ball he lined up on as long as he got to play. © *Brace Photo*

Once in a while, I got up to 190. I never played at more than that. Now the only guy on the field who weighs as little as that is the kicker."

Caroline said he enjoyed playing for George Halas, even if the boss of the Bears was a tough guy who never worried about sparing his players' feelings. Mr. Sensitivity he was not. Halas had a flavorful vocabulary, and he wasn't afraid to use it.

"He was kind of a hardnosed coach, but if you did your job, he'd take care of you," Caroline said. "He let you know what you were doing right and what you were doing wrong. He didn't yell at us all of the time. But if you were not doing what you were supposed to be doing, he'd let you know. If you needed his help off the field, he would help you. But he was going to be tough on the field because there was a ballgame out there."

Facing the Giants at the end of December in 1963 required the Bears' full attention. Winning the championship was Caroline's most memorable game, but he wraps up the final game as the result of a season of defensive accomplishment, taking a big-picture outlook.

December 29, 1963

WRIGLEY FIELD
CHICAGO BEARS 14 - NEW YORK GIANTS 10
By J.C. Caroline

The defense developed an attitude and started to personalize stuff. "I'm not gonna be letting my man catch a pass. I don't want to be embarrassed in front of the fans."

You're not content with the other guy getting a pass on third-and-8 when it is third-and-10, and the quarterback is trying to throw a pass to punish you. A lot of us started taking it personally.

"They will not score on us. They will not get a first down."

Then the defensive linemen would try to put more pressure on the quarterback. They didn't want a guy like Johnny Unitas of the Colts standing back there, taking his time, and being selective about where he wanted to throw the ball.

We had seven games where we held a team to one touchdown or less. We scored 301 points and only gave up 144 points—that's a pretty good spread. Yeah, we loved those numbers.

Playing defense, it got to the point where you didn't only depend on your athletic ability—you depended on your knowledge. You learned what your opponent was going to do against you. Your speed and quickness was not always going to get you where you ought to be. Sometimes familiarity with the other player helped a lot. A guy like Raymond Berry—also with the Colts and Unitas' favorite receiver—didn't have a lot of speed. He had good quickness with his hands, but he didn't have speed. Mostly, I played man-to-man, but against Baltimore, they had more good receivers. That put more pressure on us. They almost always gave me the fastest guy to cover.

The only shutout we had in 1963 was over the Rams. We beat them 6-0. You had to have a pretty good day to hold the Rams without a score. I haven't really reminisced about the games and that stuff in a long time. It's a long time ago, 40 years. But it was pretty good since that was our only shutout. We also beat the Rams 52-14 that year. You were not going to blow out those guys too often. Sometimes you catch a team when it's down, or they make mistakes turning the ball over, but that's not going to happen too often with a good team. One of the best guys the Rams had back then was their running back, Dick Bass. He was really good, and we had to shut him down.

Before the championship game against the Giants, many people thought they might blow us out, despite our defense. They were a high-scoring team that had an explosive offense. It was very, very challenging to play the Giants because they were a good team. We made it into our kind of game. We were physical, especially on defense. We knew we had to contain them.

Back then, fans and players made a big deal about which conference you were part of, like the American League and National League in baseball. We were the Western Conference; the Giants were the Eastern Conference. We had to represent our conference. We just figured it was going to be a knock-down, drag-out kind of game. That's the way the Bears played back in those days.

The defense kind of felt it was our responsibility in a way. If our offense turned over the ball, going onto the field we didn't go out there thinking, "The offense did this and the offense did that." It was, "Hey, let's play ball." If the Giants got good field position after a turnover, we thought, "Let's take it back." We aimed to cut them off and make them try for a field goal. Or to try to block the field goal. We weren't taking it for granted they were going to score just because they had good field position.

They had a reputation for moving the ball. They had a good ball club. It went right down to the end when we intercepted a pass. We had a pretty normal celebration after the game, not a big party. Half the time if you stayed in the same city, you got together with guys from the other team, too, because you knew them from college.

But we were the world champions.

***

Caroline played his entire pro career with the Bears, common in the 1950s and 1960s before players earned the right of free agency. Often, the core of teams stayed together for years. Management looked at it as stability to build around. Fans liked having the same guys in their town year after year with only a small amount of roster change. Caroline played at a time when the NFL began to undergo major changes. The game's popularity took a quantum leap after the so-called "greatest game ever played" between the Giants and Colts in the 1958 championship game.

"I think there was a little bit more exposure in the late 1950s," Caroline said. "Through television and getting bigger crowds."

The Green Bay Packers and Detroit Lions were prime Bears rivals during Caroline's career, but almost forgotten is another rival—the old Chicago Cardinals. The Cardinals franchise is still part of the NFL, playing out of Arizona now. Prior to the move to the desert, the team was located for decades in St. Louis. But the team was founded in Chicago and stayed there until the 1960s.

"We had a lot of guys who played against each other in college and then went on to pro teams we saw all of the time," Caroline said. "We got a little bit competitive with the Chicago Cardinals on the south side. It was like playing guys from the neighborhood. Just like you might feel with your brother, we really wanted to prove to those guys that we were better than they were. Even though we were in different conferences, you still had two teams in the same town. It's just like the Cubs and the White Sox in baseball. If you have two teams in the same town, it just makes for complications. This game is on the home court either way.

"One of the chief rivals there was Ollie Matson, who was a close friend of mine. Ollie was a tremendous athlete. He ran the quarter-mile in the Olympics. You would fight like heck on the field and fans didn't realize it, but after the game was over, we would go to the same affairs and socialize."

Caroline played more defense than offense in the NFL, but he enjoyed his stints on the other side of the ball. Most defenders fantasize about a chance to pick up a loose ball and run. He was penciled in officially and got the chance to do so on plays called by the coach and quarterback.

"It didn't make much difference to me where I played," Caroline said. "I always played defense. In the pros, I didn't expect to carry the ball a lot even when I was on offense. I did a lot of blocking stuff when I was in there. I liked hitting guys on defense."

Most pro football teams are measured by their offensive production. Fans and sportswriters always remember and highlight the big plays, the long yardage, the spectacular touchdowns. Often, keeping track of defensive statistics, absorbing defensive nuances, is overlooked until the final gun sounds and the scoreboard reflects just a handful of points for the other guys.

"In 1963, the fans seemed to recognize it before the media that we were holding opponents without touchdowns game after game," Caroline said. "We knew what we were doing, and it motivated us. A lot of times people give praise to the offense because they catch the ball or run with the ball to score a touchdown. But the defense started getting praise. We started saying out loud that we were going to make it hard for the other team to score against us. Then the fans started feeding into it. They would motivate us, too.

"Just because the offense didn't score a lot of points or take advantage of a specific situation, it didn't mean that you were going to walk away disappointed. We took real pride in trying to keep guys from scoring."

Now in his 70s, Caroline is retired from high school teaching and coaching, but he still has close relationships with school employees.

"In fact, I've still got keys to the garage," he said. "When I want to work on my car, I take it over there to the shop."

When Illinois plays football or basketball, or when the Bears play, Caroline is usually glued to the television set—if the Sunday games don't interfere with his church going or his church work.

"I still support the Bears," Caroline said. "I probably get to one game a year to stay in touch."

The rest of the time he is an armchair quarterback, like so many other Bears fans. As the 2005 season began, Caroline sensed a reasonable possibility of a Chicago turnaround, of the club putting more wins on the board than at any time since 2001. He liked the look of the young roster.

"I think they've got some pretty good athletes," Caroline said. "So it's just a matter of a break here or there. I think they'll be okay."

The man knew what he was talking about—soon after Caroline issued his evaluation, the Bears were on their way to a divisional championship for the first time in four years, and a bye in the playoffs to boot. They didn't have anybody playing both offense and defense, though, the way J.C. Caroline did in the old days.

9

ROSEY TAYLOR

afety Roosevelt Taylor's nine interceptions for the Chicago Bears during the 1963 season were the most any defender had ever swiped in team history. What made the number more memorable was that the record stood until 1991, when Mark Carrier broke it with 10 interceptions.

Taylor was nimble and swift, and like all first-class defensive backfield coverage men, he had a knack for placing himself between the quarterback and the end and taking over for the intended receiver. Taylor was in his third season as a professional the year the Bears won the title, and it was his most productive year on the field.

Those big takeaways lingered in memory for all of Taylor's teammates. On a radio show—when the Bears had a 25th-anniversary championship reunion in 1988—center Mike Pyle asked Taylor how many interceptions he had that year. When Taylor replied that he had nine, defensive tackle Fred Williams broke in and teased quarterback Bill Wade.

"Geez, that's more passes than you completed, Bill," Williams joked.

There was always a rivalry of sorts between the offense and defense on the championship team. The defense was setting records, and the offense had limited explosiveness.

"In 1963, we felt our offense didn't really come up to snuff, and the defense carried the team," Taylor said in 2004.

There was a belief the 1963 title team would win again the next year, possibly because the offense figured to be improved. Much was riding on the emergence of talented halfback Willie Galimore, but he was killed in a training camp automobile accident along with end John Farrington, and the tragedy fractured the team.

"We anticipated a lot from the offense," Taylor said. "We felt we could easily repeat. The 1963 team has been given so little credit [in all-time notoriety], but we did so many things nobody's touched since."

Specifically, Taylor spoke of the team's 36 interceptions in a 14-game season.

"If it was done nowadays," he said in 2004, "they'd be America's team."

In Chicago, the Bears of '63 are still one of the city's teams of special note. It hardly seemed possible to Taylor that 42 years had passed between the time the crown was bestowed and the time he was reminiscing about it. It was as if the years had meshed together. Forty-two years?

"Wow," he said.

Taylor was born July 4, 1937, in New Orleans, where he attended Joseph S. Clark High School. An outstanding high school player, Taylor came of age when blacks were not being recruited to compete at the major schools of the Southeastern Conference or the old Southwest Conference. Segregation still ruled all walks of life in the American south, including sports teams.

The best opportunities to play high-quality college football and to be noticed for the professional game came from signing to suit up for the traditionally black schools of the region. Over the years, Florida A&M, Tennessee State, Alcorn A&M, Bethune Cookman, and others

Rosey Taylor broke into the Bears lineup in 1961 as a kickoff man with a superb 27 yards per return average. As a safety during the 1963 title year, Taylor intercepted nine passes—a team record that stood for 28 years. © *Brace Photo*

had fielded stellar teams. No school with a traditionally black student body excelled as distinctly and memorably as Grambling State, however, under the guidance of legendary coach Eddie Robinson.

Year after year, the small Louisiana school dressed out fabulous football teams with ballplayers who made names for themselves in the National Football League. That's where Rosey Taylor matriculated in the late 1950s. The 5-foot-11, 186-pound defender with sticky fingers joined the Bears for the 1961 season. For a time, Taylor thought his new employer was more interested in using him to convince old Grambling teammate Ernie Ladd to sign with Chicago.

Ladd was a huge defensive tackle who promised to be a difference-maker for any team that chose him. Unfortunately for the Bears, the 300-pound behemoth signed with the San Diego Chargers of the American Football League and became their stalwart.

"I found out later they only signed me trying to influence Ernie Ladd to sign with them," Taylor said. "I think they got a pretty good deal with me."

Taylor proved to be a terrific bargain. As a rookie in 1961, he was a hugely successful kickoff returner, averaging 27.1 yards per runback. He stayed with the Bears until midway through the 1969 season, when he was traded to the San Francisco 49ers.

"I still hear about that when I go to Chicago and hang out with the boys," Taylor said. "All of us got along great. I don't think I've ever had a squabble or anything with anybody. They talk about the worst trade the Bears ever made, trading me in mid-season for Howard Mudd."

Taylor spent two and a half seasons with the 49ers and wrapped up his career in 1972 with the Washington Redskins. In 1970 and 1971, Taylor was in the lineup for the 49ers when they won divisional playoff games and then lost conference championship games. The big wins were 17-14 over the Minnesota Vikings the first year and 24-20 over Washington the second time.

"I was on the 49ers teams that made their first tentative efforts towards the Super Bowl," Taylor said. "They had never won anything. They were doormats."

But Taylor, whose son Brian followed him into the NFL and played parts of a few seasons beginning in 1989 with the Bears and other teams, considers himself a Bear first and foremost and roots for the team now. That's why the game of his life is the 1963 championship team's victory, culminating his best season in the sport.

December 29, 1963

WRIGLEY FIELD
CHICAGO BEARS 14 - NEW YORK GIANTS 10
By Roosevelt Taylor

The game was close, so there was some drama to it. But I was a young kid from down south and Grambling. It probably wasn't as exciting to me as it was to other older players who really realized how great a thing we had accomplished. That was my third year. Later, you understand better.

As you get older, you do enough to see and you feel things that you didn't when you were young—how important and how great a task it was. I feel that way nowadays. That was especially the case because the Bears had not won a championship for so long at the time (17 years). And the Bears have only won one championship since then (22 years later). That's a long time, and it shows you how precious they are to come by.

I don't remember individual plays, and I didn't feel the emotion at the time, but I do feel proud to be a member of that championship team. And people in Chicago do remember us. I was in Chicago for three days in 2005 going through town, signing autographs and talking to crowds about the good old days and telling stories.

No other game stands out to me, but a lot of them were special. It was just awfully exciting to play every week. Every game I was just one of the guys, and it was a lot of fun to me to be playing. I was always bouncing around. I don't know if you're familiar with the way I played. It's a fact, I bounced all over the field. I played basketball all over the football field.

I would like to think I made a statement in Chicago, not just being part of the championship team and playing in that famous game, but I was out there every second when I was with the Bears. In eight and a half years with the Bears, I didn't miss a single game. I didn't miss a single game of pro football until my last year.

***

Taylor said he didn't know anything about the Bears when he joined the team, just that he was going to the pros. The Bears treated him well until the trade, and he enjoyed himself in Chicago.

"They gave me the break to play professional football," Taylor said, "and all of the knowledge I grabbed in those years, I got it while with the Bears. When I left the Bears, I was considered an old-timer with the 49ers. It was my ninth year."

Taylor had the remarkably fortuitous timing to go from playing under Eddie Robinson, who became the winningest college coach, to playing under George Halas, who was the winningest professional coach until Don Shula broke his record. That is quite the double play with football history.

Robinson knew how to raise his voice a few decibels himself, but he was considered a bit more courtly than his northern counterpart. Taylor believes that he and Frank Cornish, a defensive tackle who joined the Bears in 1966 out of Grambling, were the only two who experienced a direct Robinson-Halas pipeline.

Halas was demonstrative; he cussed constantly; he was a devil of a negotiator; he screamed at officials; and he practically sprinted up and down the sidelines while his team played. He was one of a kind, whether a young man who had been exposed to few other coaches knew it or not.

"Halas simply was the National Football League," Taylor said. "I hadn't met that many people in my life and certainly not millionaires from a big city. Everything he did just amused or amazed me— everything he did or said."

Taylor had little frame of reference for Halas, the Chicago Bears, or even professional football where he grew up. Pro football was integrated thoroughly by 1961, but that didn't mean a young man from New Orleans who played at Grambling personally knew anybody who had followed the path.

"I really didn't have any expectations when I went to Chicago because I'd never been around a guy who had played professional football," Taylor said. "From this whole city of New Orleans and the whole southern part of Louisiana, I don't think there had been an African-American yet to play in the National Football League. The only Grambling guy who had come along before me to make a name in the NFL by then was Tank Younger."

Younger, whose given name was Paul, broke into the NFL in 1949 and played with the Los Angeles Rams until 1958 when he retired with a 4.7 yards-per-carry record as an outstanding fullback. The massive lineman Buck Buchanan, a friend and teammate, followed Taylor into the NFL from Grambling in 1963 and reached the Hall of Fame in 1990 after a long career with the Kansas City Chiefs.

The player Taylor was most proud of following him into the NFL was his son Brian who also attended high school in New Orleans and played collegiate ball at Oregon State. The younger Taylor, though, did not have his father's pro longevity.

"My son only played four years and blew his knee out," Taylor said. "He had to have a couple of operations."

Taylor said he was fortunate not to experience severe injuries during his 12 seasons in the league.

"I just loved playing," Taylor said. "I enjoyed it. It was just wonderful to be able to do it as well as I could. You kind of compare yourself to other people, I think, and if you believe everybody, I was a pretty good player. I felt great all the time. I didn't have all of those injuries. If I had had injuries it would have been slightly different. I was one of the lucky ones."

As the Bears began the 2005 season—one that would play out surprisingly well for them given doom-and-gloom summer predictions—Taylor made it clear who he gives his allegiance to in the annual race to the Super Bowl.

"I'd like the Bears to win it," he said. "Maybe it's because of sentimental reasons."

As Taylor has learned through the passage of time, championships notched early in a career stay with a player forever. When you are one of the guys with a title on your resume, it lasts. The Bears won that 1963 title more than 40 years ago and yet Chicagoans can still tell you. "That Rosey Taylor, he was a heck of a defensive back. Boy, did he intercept a lot of passes."

Yes, he was—and yes, he did.

10

JOE FORTUNATO

O ne of the many great linebackers who frequented the Chicago Bears' lineup, Joe Fortunato remains a popular sports figure in Mississippi, where he attended Mississippi State and was a top Southeastern Conference player.

Fortunato was born March 28, 1930, in Mingo Junction, Ohio, and grew up there. After playing collegiate football at Virginia Military before transferring to Mississippi State, Fortunato spent his entire National Football League career with the Bears between 1955 and 1966, then moved back to the south.

Fortunato may be in his mid-70s, but he is not retired. He lives in Natchez and operates an oil-and-gas exploration outfit.

"We put prospects together, and I get out and raise the money and we drill," Fortunato said.

That's one kind of drilling he engages in—truth be told, Fortunato has almost as much invested in prospecting for fish. The high-quality fishing life offered is one thing that attracted him to Mississippi. On the occasions he boats offshore, he'll chase speckled trout and redfish, maybe even a shark or two.

Fortunato, who played at 6 feet, 1 inch, and 225 pounds, is about as avid an outdoorsman as he was a football player. He used to hunt often, but now focuses on fishing. He expounds on his passion for angling with the same enthusiasm that emphasizes his favorite moments on the gridiron.

"I have a place that's a couple of hundred acres," Fortunato said, "and it's got a 45-acre lake on it. I'll tell you what, the fishing is as good as you can get. We go after brim and bass, and we can fly fish if we want. We can cast, but I like to fish with a cane pole with a cork and a cricket on the end. In Natchez, Mississippi, the surrounding area is a tremendous place for fishing and hunting. Boy, the deer hunting down here is unbelievable—deer hunting, squirrels, dove, anything.

"The shark fishing is on the Gulf of Mexico, offshore, but around here, you might find an alligator or a big tarpon, too. Anyone who comes down to visit, I take his butt fishing."

Fortunato makes it sound impossible to stay landlocked once you set foot on his property. He'll talk football with a fishing rod in one hand.

Fortunato was drafted out of college in the seventh round by the Bears in 1952, but he had a military commitment and did not join the team until three years later. Once he stepped into the starting lineup, he anchored one of the outside linebacker positions for more than a decade. Fortunato teamed up with the great Bill George and Larry Morris to form one of the most impressive Bears linebacking trios of all-time.

Ferocious tacklers, the threesome helped the front four put pressure on the quarterback and agilely dropped back into pass coverage and picked off errant throws. Fortunato intercepted 16 passes in his career, three each in 1961 and 1962. Fortunato took tremendous pleasure in the success of the linebackers as a group because the pieces fit so efficiently together.

"It sure was a great trio," he said. "We played together so well."

Fortunato joined the Bears in 1955, a year before they made it to the NFL title game for the first time in 10 years. The Bears finished 8-

When he wasn't fishing, Joe Fortunato was tackling enemy runners or quarterbacks. A rugged linebacker whom coach George Halas trusted to call defensive signals, Fortunato spent his entire pro football career with the Bears. © *Brace Photo*

4 that season, and during most of Fortunato's playing days (he never played for another team), the club was a contender. He was also a key performer on the 1963 championship team.

When he gave up playing, Fortunato stayed with the Bears for two seasons, 1967 and 1968, as an assistant coach. To Fortunato—just like all the other teammates who lived through that time and captured only a single title—winning the 1963 championship was the pinnacle of his career. But a game that preceded it that season, one that set up the Bears' place in the championship game, provided a special memory of what he thinks of as his favorite game. The Bears had already beaten the Packers once that season and wanted to drive a stake in their hearts to prevent the archrivals from sneaking into first place and claiming the Bears' playoff spot.

November 17, 1963

WRIGLEY FIELD
CHICAGO BEARS 26 - GREEN BAY PACKERS 7
By Joe Fortunato

We were up in the standings, and we wanted to stay there. We had the advantage of beating the Packers already; but if they beat us, they would tie us. They could still go to the championship game instead of us.

The night before the game I was studying my defensive plays. I was calling the defensive signals then with Bill George and Larry Morris. We were worried about the game. It was about midnight when the phone rang. George Halas called me. I don't know why he called me so damned late. The way he acted, he must have been nervous.

"Joe, I've gotta ask you something. How's everything coming? How's the signals look?" He is talking this and that and everything.

"Coach," I said. "I was still up when you called me. I was just about to finish up. The way the charts look, if they continue to do what they've been doing, we may shut them out."

Halas didn't say anything for a few seconds, and I said, "We're going to do a good job, and we'll beat them defensively." Halas liked to hear the guys talk like that, to show confidence and stuff. The next day at Wrigley Field, we did almost shut them out. It was 26-7, and they only scored in the last few seconds of the game. The game went just like I thought it could. These were the Packers of Bart Starr, Paul Hornung, and Jim Taylor, and they had all of those good linemen. They were the ones who had been shutting people out. Once we won that game, I knew the Packers were not going to catch us, and I knew we were going to play for the world championship.

We all had good games, but the defense had a great game. We had a great defense in 1963. We finished the regular season 11-1-2. Beating the Packers twice was icing on the cake. The Packers were all the rage at that time under Vince Lombardi, and they did a lot of winning in the 1960s. But that year, it was our turn, and that was the game that set it up in my mind.

Fortunato played for the Bears in 1956, the most recent previous time they had advanced to the championship game. The 47-7 loss to the New York Giants stung at the time, and it was like a festering wound among the Bears who remained on the roster for several years. When the 1963 Bears realized they were going to get a chance at avenging themselves against the Giants they were particularly revved up.

To win a championship without considering it a paramount moment in your career is impossible; and Fortunato counts that triumph as the latter of the two greatest games of his Bears life.

December 29, 1963

WRIGLEY FIELD
CHICAGO BEARS 14 - NEW YORK GIANTS 10
By Joe Fortunato

We were pretty hyped up to play the Giants. The main reason was the loss in 1956 when they beat the hell out of us in New York. They had the tennis shoes; and we were sliding all over in cleats. Everybody remembered that game. All of us wanted to take our frustration from that game out on them and make sure they had the same thing happen to them. We wanted them to feel badly about losing to us, so we were all really fired up going into the game.

On the day of the game, I was nervous because it was a big game and because I was calling the signals. I was up late the night before that game, too, worrying if I had everything down pat. I had to memorize the right signals to call in certain situations. When we began to play I was less nervous, and everything was working out really well. It was a really close game, but we intercepted Y.A. Tittle five times, so I would have to say the defense did its job. One after the other, we picked off passes, knocking the Giants' defense out of its rhythm.

I didn't play one of my best games, but I was okay. I didn't make many tackles. But collectively, the defense played a helluva ball game.

After we won, after we celebrated, I stayed up late that night watching the game film. When I was coaching for the Bears after I retired, I'd watch it sometimes, too. Then I didn't see it for 35 years. My son, Mike, who lives in Atlanta, found a copy of the game on eBay in 2005, bought it, and sent it to me, so I finally watched it again.

Watching the film, I laughed a lot because looking at yourself and all of your friends so long ago, it kind of makes you wonder if that is really you. It brought back a lot of old memories, I can tell you that. The film was a fun thing to get.

I was married to my first wife for 46 years, and she died about six years ago. I got married again about three years later, and my second wife, Catherine, had never been around for my football career. She hadn't seen the championship game, and we watched it together. I'll tell you, it was interesting to watch it with her. She laughed at me on the field and the way I ran, and teased me about all kinds of stuff like that.

***

Fortunato said the guys who shared the glory of the 1963 championship were a particularly close-knit group. They were warm to one another at the time, a warmth that has lingered over the years. Only the day before he had chatted with defensive end Doug Atkins on the phone. Periodically, he makes trips to Chicago to participate in old-timers events, to attend dinners and reunions and sign autographs. Fortunato always finds it a pleasure to spend time with the men who have the common bond of being members of a Bears title team.

"We really had a lot of camaraderie," Fortunato said. "A lot of teams don't have that, but we had it. We didn't have all of the best players, but we had players who gave 110 percent and did a helluva job."

For Fortunato, those are times to cherish because he has little in the way of souvenirs from his playing days. When he was younger, he tried to preserve some memorabilia, but some years ago he put it aside in a safe place that turned out not to be so safe.

"What happend was that we had all the stuff stored, and the building burned," Fortunato said. "Not long ago someone asked me for a picture to use for an award they were giving me. I tried to find something, and I could not find anything. Most of the stuff burned up. Around that time, the athletic director at Mississippi State was going through some of his old stuff and he found a picture of me and sent it to me. So I have that. That's the only old picture I have."

Fortunato marvels at the amount of interest in his playing days, the Bears of old and the championship squad. He said he gets more attention now than when he was active. Although he always appreciated the fans of Chicago and enjoyed the city, he did not make regular visits back for a long time.

When Fortunato married Catherine, however, he began going back to Chicago. She wanted to go on the trips. When invites came, she urged him to participate.

"We've been to Chicago four times in the last year," Fortunato said in the summer of 2005. He joked that sometimes he has to hide invitations from the Mrs. so he can stay home in Mississippi once in a while instead of taking another journey to Chicago.

Mostly, though, you can count on Fortunato being on hand for any Bears event that allows him to mingle with his once-upon-a-time teammates and brings him near to the only team he knew as a pro. The passing years never changed one thing: Fortunato has been a Bears fan from afar and is a Bears fan today.

"Hell, yes, I root for the Bears," he said. "I'm a diehard Bears fan. I was associated with the team for 14 years. There's no other team but the Bears, as far as I'm concerned."

11

GALE SAYERS

None of us will ever truly know how much it hurt Gale Sayers to have his career shut down; to possess, innately, what many thought was the greatest natural ability and instinct in a running back, only to see it destroyed prematurely.

He is not a man who would ever be a likely candidate as an Oprah guest to pour out his heart. He is not a man given to public wailing. Sayers lived out a pro football career long enough to leave those who saw him play with mental photographs of brilliance. The "Kansas Comet," as Sayers was nicknamed during his college playing days, was a streak of lightning. He was a dancer with the feet of Fred Astaire. He was the dawn of a new era—a glimpse of the future before the door was slammed shut for years. He could run like an antelope in the open field, and slash through narrow openings in the defensive line the way a deer darted through the woods, making the branches bend for him.

Sayers never said he was the greatest player ever to tote a pigskin, but he admitted he was flattered when experts and observers put him on the short list alongside Jim Brown, O.J. Simpson, Walter Payton, Barry Sanders, and Emmitt Smith. If four decades after his retirement Brown remains the best football player of all time, clear consensus has determined who would line up next to him in the backfield. Yet Sayers made his imprint in many fewer carries, over fewer seasons, with the least number of opportunities of any of the others. Numbers tell the story of longevity and accomplishment among running backs, and all of the others' numbers are bigger. None of the others had the bad luck Sayers suffered—the first knee injury slowed him in the ninth game of the 1968 season, and the next knee injury, in 1970, finished him all too soon.

The witnesses will die off and it will become evermore difficult for those who never saw Sayers play live nor on tape to determine his worth because his numbers are limited. Suffice to say—and many have—Sayers owned the magnificent characteristic of greatness in his swift legs and his swift mind, and you had to see it to appreciate it, had to see it to *believe* it. Early on, he was nicknamed "Black Magic" for his slick moves on the field.

Gale Sayers was born May 30, 1943, in Wichita, Kansas. He attended high school in Omaha, Nebraska, and played collegiate ball for the University of Kansas, where he developed a galaxy of admirers around the old Big Eight Conference and became a two-time All-American.

When Sayers was drafted by the Bears—one of their two No. 1 picks in 1965—he became a disciple of owner George Halas. From the get-go, Halas told Sayers how special he was, later saying, "He was the best I ever saw." But he also warned Sayers to make sure he used every off-field moment to prepare for a life after football. That is a hard lesson to absorb for young players with great promise before them and an apparently long career ahead of them. Yet Sayers listened, and when his career was cut short, he was not caught adrift.

Halas not only recognized Sayers' great talent, but he recognized traits in Sayers the player himself did not at first see. Halas made the revolutionary move of putting Sayers together with another running back as road roommates. Nothing surprising about that—however, Sayers is black, and Brian Piccolo was white. Race mixing never had been tried in major American professional sports, but the men were compatible and became good friends.

Gale Sayers never let rain and mud slow him down. In his brief Bears career as a halfback, cut short by injuries, Sayers was a touchdown machine. He was the youngest player enshrined in the Hall of Fame. *Photo by Diamond Images/Getty Images*

When Sayers wrote an early autobiography called *I Am Third*, a chapter highlighting Piccolo's tragic death from cancer was singled out and made into a highly popular and critically acclaimed television movie called *Brian's Song*. For more than 40 years, the relationship has lingered in the public mind, and the film has remained one of the most praised sports-related movies of all time.

In *I Am Third*, which was republished recently with a fresh introduction from Sayers, he looks back on life from a very different perspective, and wrote that he and Piccolo always joked about race and occasionally put interviewers on. After a brief feeling-out period, they never thought much about it, he said.

Piccolo, who was only 26 when he died, was an active player when he became ill. The first signs were a nagging cough, and his decline was remarkably swift despite numerous surgeries. Sayers was not even able to be with Piccolo when he died. Sayers' parents were hospitalized with injuries suffered in an automobile crash, and then Sayers became ill and was hospitalized himself.

The 6-foot-tall Sayers, who played at just under 200 pounds, had been a sleek, nearly perfect athlete, with no flaws, and his physical abilities had made him king on the field in high school and college. When he first suffered a knee injury, Sayers retreated into a shell of depression and self-doubt. Like so many athletes, he had measured his self-worth only by sporting accomplishments and never had cause to doubt himself.

Over time Sayers became more mature. His entire professional football career lasted only seven seasons between 1965 and 1971, but he was really only healthy for roughly three and a half of them. His career rushing total was 4,956 yards, but he averaged 5.0 yards per carry, a more accurate indicator of his special skills. Sayers' best year running from scrimmage was 1966, when he rushed for 1,231 yards. Sayers also ran a kickoff back a team-record 103 yards during a game against the Pittsburgh Steelers in 1967.

Sayers was something to behold as a rookie when he set a National Football League record of 22 touchdowns in a 14-game season through runs, pass catches, and returns. Sayers was the Bears' pre-eminent weapon that season, capable of scoring any way from anywhere on the field when he cradled his hands on the ball. He was voted rookie of the year unanimously.

The most stunning day of Sayers' debut season—any rookie's, really—occurred on a soggy, muddy field, when he scored a league record-tying six touchdowns in a single game. When Sayers ran that day, he splashed along. Remarkably, he could keep his footing, and as he threw up water and dirt on his pursuers like a car splashing trailing windshields, he made his normal, hard-to-follow cuts that confused tacklers. The touchdowns came on a 65-yard punt return, an 80-yard pass play, and runs of 50 yards, 21, 7, and one yards. The showing matched the records of Ernie Nevers and Dub Jones. That day, Sayers seemed to be wearing ruby slippers.

December 12, 1965

WRIGLEY FIELD
CHICAGO BEARS 61 - SAN FRANCISCO 49ERS 20
By Gale Sayers

No magic shoes.

You know, if it's muddy like that, and everybody wears four-inch cleats, they can drive through it. Mud will fill in between cleats, but not everybody wore them. It just seemed like everybody was slipping but me. It was a very, very rainy day.

On the third play of that game, quarterback Rudy Bukich threw me a swing pass, and I went 80 yards—and it seemed everyone was tripping. After that, it was just the Bears' game. We could do nothing wrong. When I was driving from my house to the game, I thought the game might be 14-7 or 21-7. There are usually certain things you can't do in a game like that. Usually you can't run very well because you're slipping and sliding. You just pray you can make the plays to win.

I could do nothing wrong that day, either. I hadn't put much stock in it being such a special game, not one of the great games in NFL history. The commissioner had called me that morning and said, "Gale, they are pushing Ken Willard [the 49ers fullback] for rookie of the year. You should try to have a decent game." I didn't think that much about it after he talked to me. I didn't think anything about it. I went out there and played my game and did what I had to do.

We just didn't think about records back then. I didn't think about records. I figured that, when the score was about 30-10, I was coming out. If we had talked about a record on the sidelines, I probably could have scored nine touchdowns.

People always say you get into a zone when everything is going so well—Michael Jordan is in a zone when he's shooting well. Well, there is no zone. You play ball. You were playing a game, saying that day, "Hey, I played the game very, very well." The whole team played well because I had to have some blocking or there were no touchdowns. I didn't do it by myself. Somebody had to block, somebody had to do something so I could cut one way or cut another way to score a touchdown. So I didn't think anything about "Gale, you're in a zone. You can do anything you want to do today." No, it was nothing like that.

We were just going well as an offense and the defense, essentially they held the 49ers so we could get the ball back and score. The only thing we were concerned with was playing the ballgame. When the game ended, people let me know what I had done, but my rookie year I was a very, very shy individual. I didn't think about how special it was. They said, "You've got a record." I thought, "Big deal." Somebody asked me if it was my best game ever. But being a football player going back to grade school, high school and college, I said no. When I played midget football, I scored seven touchdowns in a game. I just wanted to let it go.

That was some revenge, though. It was a great game for us. In the first game of the season, the 49ers beat us 52-24. Before the game, Coach Halas talked about that. He said, "In the first football game of the season, they whipped your ass, 52-24. Let's go out there and see what we can do."

Damned right, Halas would play up those things to get the players going. During the course of the week, the coaches wouldn't let up. They put things on the wall like "49ers first game, 52-24." They did things like that to motivate you.

We were also going very well at that point in the season, and we felt if we won the rest of our games, we could win the Western Division championship—which was also in the equation.

Sayers played at one of the periods of time when the Bears and Packers conflicts were at their zenith in terms of intensity.

"Coach Halas always played up the Green Bay games," Sayers said. "So did assistant coach Jim Dooley and the other coaches—you knew you had to beat the Packers. It's the oldest rivalry in the league. Back then we didn't have free agents switching teams, so you would have players on the team for six, seven, eight years, so they really understood the rivalry. Now guys play on a team for two years and they go. They don't understand a rivalry like that. We knew about it, and the coaches talked about it and said, "We've got to beat those bastards." The Packers had a great team, but we didn't care what the record was, we felt, "Hey, it's going to be a helluva game." My whole career it seemed like they would beat us in Green Bay and we would beat them in Chicago.

"I liked it when the Bears' new coach, Lovie Smith, took over and said it was a goal to beat the Packers. He knows history, and players today don't care about history. They want to know how much money they can make. But back then, the Bears-Packers rivalry was the biggest rivalry in the NFL."

At various times over the years, Sayers has been asked which defensive standouts of the period hit hardest. He cites Packers linebacker Ray Nitschke, Lions linebacker Joe Schmidt, and Rams defensive end Deacon Jones as guys who knew how to bring it. But he always says that his own teammate, Dick Butkus, a first-round draft pick the same year Sayers was taken, outdid them all in practice.

One of the aspects of being a Bear in the 1960s that Sayers most enjoyed was playing home games at Wrigley Field.

"You know, with 48,000 people in the building, they're right there on top of you, and that was a real home-field advantage," he said. "It was a really great place to play. Too bad they had to go to Soldier Field, but that's the history of the league. They want to move to bigger places that seat more than 50,000 people. You couldn't get 50,000 into Wrigley Field no matter what, but it was a great, great place to play."

Sayers' lukewarm feelings about Soldier Field aside, whenever he is in town during the fall and the Bears are too, he heads to the stadium.

"I go to every game that I can," he said.

Sayers' career was so short that he was retired before he turned 30 years old. It also meant that at 34 he was the youngest-ever inductee to the Pro Football Hall of Fame. Among the things he did after his retirement from pro football, Sayers acted as assistant athletic director at his alma mater (clicking those cleats together took him back to Kansas after all), took over as athletic director at Southern Illinois University, and then went into private business in the suburbs of Chicago, where he still lives. For the last quarter-century, Sayers has owned a computer company that distributes hardware, software, and provides all types of services and support. Periodically, he attends Bears-related events or makes autograph signing appearances in the region.

"This is a Bears town," Sayers said. "No question about it, you're always a Bear, and first and foremost they care about their Bears."

12

DOUG BUFFONE

G iven the timeframe of Doug Buffone's career and his longevity, playing linebacker for the Bears between 1966 and 1979, he competed alongside overlapping generations of team greats.

At various times, Buffone was a teammate of Doug Atkins and Joe Fortunato, top defenders from the 1963 title team, star tight end Mike Ditka, the future Super Bowl coach, Dick Butkus and Gale Sayers of the late 1960s-early 1970s era, and superstar Walter Payton of the Super Bowl bunch. Alas, Buffone came along precisely in the middle of the period between Bears world championships, so he never earned a ring.

Buffone was a youngster with some of those players, a peer of others, and a veteran with the last group.

"Joe taught me," Buffone said of Fortunato. "I was a left-side linebacker, and Joe was a left-side linebacker. When I came up, I learned from him; and then when Joe retired, I took his spot."

Fortunato, who lives in Mississippi, had a reputation as a first-rate fisherman even when he was playing.

"He's got a place down there, and he's got a gigantic lake on it," Buffone said. "He's real good at fishing. He's just Mr. Southerner."

Douglas John Buffone was born June 27, 1944, in Yatesboro, Pennsylvania. He played football for Shannock Valley High School and then competed at the University of Louisville before becoming a fourth-round draft pick of the Bears in 1966. Buffone is 6 feet 3 inches and played at 230 pounds, an above-average-sized linebacker for the time period.

Buffone, who spent his entire National Football League career in Chicago, was one player who got his first taste of the Bears-Green Bay Packers rivalry, and an early education before he even put on his first Bears uni. In the '60s, a preseason college all-star game was still contested, pitting the stars of the graduating senior class against the defending NFL champion.

"The rivalry was emphasized more when I first came up," Buffone said. "The all-stars were playing the champion of the previous year, and in 1966, that was the Green Bay Packers. So I played against them in the all-star game.

"Then I go to training camp with the Bears, and we had to play the Packers in an exhibition game. And then two more games in the regular season. It didn't take me long to see what was going on. It really was nuts because we were playing the Packers. That's just the way it was. We called it 'Packer Panic Week'. I think over time it's lessened some. Lately, I don't think the fans have forgotten, but I think the players have. A lot of them will say it's just another game, but it definitely wasn't when I was playing."

Buffone was a mainstay at linebacker for the Bears for 186 games, during which he collected 24 interceptions. He was best known for his hard-nosed tackling, but he was glad that he didn't have to tackle the two great running backs he teamed with during his Bears career.

"Walter Payton was terrific," Buffone said. "I played four years with Walter; and I also played four years with Gale Sayers. I was lucky to be in that position. You try to compare them, but they're both great.

"Gale was probably the most elusive runner. We used to call him 'Magic'. The guy would disappear. Walter would take three people

Linebacker Doug Buffone had a long and successful career with the Bears, playing in 186 games for the team and competing in both Wrigley Field and Soldier Field.
Photo by Bruce Bennett Studios/Getty Images

with him. Walter was a better blocker, too. Gale was a tremendous, tremendous kickoff and punt returner. Both of these guys, in my mind, are probably the two best backs who ever played.

"I went through all kinds of stuff with the Bears, some of it good, and some of it bad when we were losing. But I don't know how many Hall of Famers I played with. Nine? Ten?"

Although Buffone did not get the chance to play on either of the legendary teams that bracketed his career with the Bears, he did find himself on the field for one truly memorable team miracle that he considers the game of his life.

December 16, 1979

SOLDIER FIELD
CHICAGO BEARS 42 - ST. LOUIS CARDINALS 6
By Doug Buffone

The best game I think I played, one that really meant something, actually took place in my last year. The key to that whole game was simple. We were 9-6, but the way the standings were set up, we had to win by 32 points, and the Dallas Cowboys had to beat the Washington Redskins, for us to get into the playoffs.

Everybody knew all week with the tiebreakers it wasn't just enough for us to win, we had to annihilate St. Louis. The fans, the writers, everybody was talking like we didn't have a chance. They said, "Stop it. You're going to beat St. Louis by 30-some points? You're gonna have Dallas beat Washington? What are you guys talking about?"

My whole career I had only been to the playoffs once (in 1977 for a first-round loss at Dallas), so it was really important to me. I thought we had a good team, a very good team, but the odds in those circumstances were against us.

What made that game so interesting was the fact that our coach, Neill Armstrong, had us playing it like we were just playing at the park. Why I say that is because we did everything. We had fake handoffs and fake punts. On a fake punt, our punter Bob Parsons threw a pass to me. I was coming out of the backfield. I ran down the sideline and caught it. That was my catch. That was the only time I caught a pass in my career. I had run out of the backfield before, but this time when we faked, it was going to be a pass. I lined up, saw the defense, and gave Bob the signal. It looked like it was going to be a screen pass. The defender was rushing. I hit him and just peeled off. Bob rolled out and hit me with the ball, and I went for 22 yards for a first down. That was his only pass completion of the year, too. We had fake field goals that day. We had fake everything.

On that day, the key for us was we could do anything, we could try anything, because we needed to win big. We just couldn't win the game 10-6 or 14-7. We had to win by more than 30 points, and we won by 36 points. Can you imagine that? We went out and did the damned thing. It was truly amazing, but we had to have the Cowboys beat Washington.

In our game, basically, we did a lot of special things. I don't have tremendous speed, but I caught a guy on punt return coverage who was running down the sidelines. I caught the son-of-a-gun. We were a good team, we finished 10-6, but we seemed to be doing things beyond our capabilities. I don't know how we did it all. It was meant to be. There's no question of the fact that when you have incentive and you put your mind to something—if something needs to be done—you can make things happen.

We won big, but it wasn't over. The Dallas and Washington game started later than ours did. When our game ended, that one was still going on. We—the players—all stayed at Soldier Field to watch it. And it was packed. People had portable television sets and stayed to watch it. And we watched that thing right out underneath the stands after we showered up!

For a while, it looked dismal. It looked bad. Then all of a sudden Dallas jumped back in there. They moved the football, scored, and then they won; and we went to the playoffs. It was just a super day. When the Dallas-Washington game ended, we were all just screaming and yelling. We had done something special. What are the odds of doing something like that? The odds are against you. You have no chance of doing that. You've got to have double the luck.

I played in a ton of games, close games, but this game, beating St. Louis, meant more than any of them. The improbability of it all was something.

That's why sports is so great. You can never count yourself out. You can say the odds are this or the odds are that and that you have no chance. But as soon as they start hearing those things, for some reason, players have a tendency to try to turn that stuff around in their favor. You might think you've seen it all, but you've never seen it all.

***

After he retired from active duty, Buffone remained in the Chicago area and embarked on a new career as a radio broadcaster. His Bears expertise and commentary were in demand, and he got paid to say whatever was on his mind about the team.

"I came to this town in 1966, and I stayed," Buffone said. "I have memories that are so great, of playing at Wrigley Field, playing at Soldier Field, playing with a lot of terrific football players."

13

MATT SUHEY

He was the other guy in the backfield, the one assigned to block more than run, the sidekick to the game's all-time leading rusher. Fullback Matt Suhey was the amazing Walter Payton's running mate, on the field and off, in football and friendship. He was comparatively unheralded as a yardage-gaining force, but his job served as a major ingredient in the making of the Bears' 1986 Super Bowl champions.

In the world of pro football today, the fullback is almost as invisible as the right guard, accumulating almost as few measurable statistics as the center who snaps the ball. The fullback is supposed to block rather than run, create holes rather than batter tacklers with his body. Matt Suhey was active with the Bears when fullbacks still counted as key members of the offensive attack rather than solely as protectors of the quarterback or the halfback. Sure they took on all comers trying to beat up their backfield friends, but they also got their own chances to advance the football.

"I caught a lot of passes, and I got involved in a lot of aspects of the game," Suhey recalled. "It's unfortunate how the role has changed. I don't know why the fullback is now almost like a lineman."

Matthew Jerome Suhey was born on July 7, 1958, in Bellefonte, Pennsylvania. He attended high school in State College, a community famous as the home base of Penn State. Suhey unsurprisingly chose to stay home and compete for the nationally respected Nittany Lions.

Suhey became a second-round draft pick of the Bears in 1980 and spent his entire NFL career between 1980 and 1989 with Chicago, most of the time sharing the backfield with Payton, who is considered one of the greatest all-around players ever to suit up. After retirement, Suhey remained in the Chicago area, where he became a successful businessman.

As a mainstay in the backfield, Suhey played a pivotal role for the 1985 Bears and throughout the ensuing playoffs. If Payton was the number-one option, Suhey was the change-of-pace back—the guy who made defenses pay when they keyed too single-mindedly on Payton. In the mid-1980s, when the Bears were at the zenith of their game, they were a run-oriented club. Payton's star outshone all others, but Suhey demonstrated that the Bears' run offense was multi-dimensional. He did an admirable job of burning teams that failed to recognize he was a critical weapon in the Bears' attack.

Suhey played in 148 games with the Bears during the 1980s and rushed for 2,946 yards. His season high was 681 yards in 1983, but he rushed for 471 yards at more than four yards per carry during the Super Bowl season. Suhey also dabbled in kickoff returns, most notably during his rookie season when he fielded 19 kicks for a 21.4 yards-per-return average. What truly caught defenses off-guard time after time, however, was Suhey's pass-catching ability. Frequently, he served as the safety valve for a quarterback ducking the rush. Seven times in his career, Suhey caught 20 or more passes in a season. In 1983, he snared 49. The contributions were invaluable to a Bears team that was known more for militarily scorching the earth one chunk of mileage at a time.

The team goal of establishing the run first and avoiding interceptions and fumbles stemmed from Coach Mike Ditka. He

Hardnosed Matt Suhey not only blocked for backfield partner Walter Payton, his close friend, but unlike the fullbacks of today, he was a dual threat, running and catching passes. *Photo by Jonathan Daniel/Getty Images*

wanted to play ball control, and Suhey's strength as a 5-foot-11, 217-pound fullback was short-yardage bursts complemented by the short-yardage passes.

"A lot of it was Mike Ditka," Suhey said, "and his philosophy to run the football, control the football, not turn the ball over. Our defense was a phenomenal defense, but the offense was very good at giving the defense rest. When they weren't out on the field they became even more overwhelming."

The Bears scored 456 points during the 1985 Super Bowl run and allowed just 198 points and dominated in time of possession. Keeping the ball out of the hands of the opposition was an effective strategy.

"How well we rushed and controlled the football was big," Suhey said. "We led the league in rushing for a number of years. The whole thing was designed to keep our defense off the field for large amounts of time."

Suhey was in the Bears lineup for a few years before the team began to remake itself into a Super Bowl contender. He first felt a foundation for something meaningful was being built late during the 8-8 season of 1983. With two games remaining in the regular season, the Bears' record was 6-8. Then came a victory that not only contained perhaps the flashiest play of Suhey's career, but a character-building, team-uplifting memory.

December 11, 1983

HUBERT H. HUMPHREY METRODOME
CHICAGO BEARS 19 - MINNESOTA VIKINGS 13
By Matt Suhey

When Mike Ditka came in, he said we were going to win the Super Bowl. It was like two different worlds from where we had been. He said a lot of the guys on the roster would be there and a lot of the guys were not going to be there. Up until then—in my first few years—the Vikings had always beat us. They were one of the teams we could never beat.

If you aspire to be a Super Bowl team, you have to pass through certain stages. You can't be losing to certain teams all of the time, and Ditka understood that. We couldn't beat the Packers for a while, either—not at all.

Against Minnesota, I threw a 74-yard touchdown pass on an option-three play that began with a lateral. We practiced it all of the time. After the hike, McMahon tossed the ball back to me. I rolled out to the right side. Usually, when we ran an option, it was a halfback option with Walter throwing the ball, often throwing it to me.

This time, Walter was running a button hook when I caught the ball. He turned and ran, and he was open, so I threw the ball to him. We were in our own territory at the 26-yard line, so it took a lot of guts to call that play. Walter was out about 20 yards when I threw it to him, and he ran the rest of the way. We were in a close game, but we had practiced it so much. It was just one of those things that turned out very well. That was the only pass I threw all year. I was one-for-one for 74 yards.

That play told us, "Maybe we could be somebody." All the teams that had beaten us over the years, we could come back and beat them. We can play with them now. We won the game, and it showed us that we could beat the Vikings. That was a step for that Bears team. Then the next week we did it again, beating the Packers; and that was a lesson, too, showing us we could beat Green Bay. The games went hand-in-hand.

December 18, 1983

SOLDIER FIELD
CHICAGO BEARS 23 - GREEN BAY PACKERS 21
By Matt Suhey

It was the last game Bart Starr coached for the Packers—and it was very, very cold. The wind-chill factor was 50 below zero, or something like that.

What made that game so special, besides beating the Packers, was that we had a late drive, maybe with two minutes left, to win the game. That was fun. The 1982 season had been messed up by the strike, we'd only won three of nine games. We were getting better, and when we played the Packers, we were coming off that great win over the Vikings. The Packers game was the first time we ever came back to win a game in my career.

Beating the Packers got us over the hump. We felt we were starting to turn things around. Bart Starr was fired, and they brought in Forrest Gregg as coach. There was always a special feeling playing the Packers, even more so when Gregg became coach. It really heated up. It really started in the 1984 preseason, when we played them in Milwaukee. We should have known it would be a war, which it was, and which is fine. With Gregg as coach, we had a guy to go to war with. It was always a very, very difficult, tough game.

Those were the building blocks; and by the time 1985 rolled around, I knew we were awfully good.

***

When fans and historians look back at the Bears of 1985, most of the focus tends to be on the defense. Suhey wants to remind those people that the offense excelled, too.

"They certainly had a lot of personalities over there," Suhey said of a defense that featured men like Mike Singletary, Steve "Mongo" McMichael, Gary Fencik, and William "The Refrigerator" Perry. "But they were phenomenal. I don't think they really overshadowed the offense, though. We had Walter Payton, and he was the key piece of that offensive unit."

That Super season, Payton rushed for 1,421 yards and caught 53 passes. As often as not, Suhey was called upon to block for him. He was "more of a change-up" in the offense when his number was called, there to catch defenders napping.

"I carried the ball eight to 10 times a game," Suhey said.

Patyon was the main man, the engine for the offense, always a threat to break a long run and one who saw the ball as often as Ditka dared to put it into his hands without leaving his star breathless.

"Walter had preparation that was second to none," Suhey said. "He was always in great, great shape. Certainly, we had a belief in his ability to deliver in difficult times and situations."

Suhey said his teammates on the other side of the ball deserved all of their accolades.

"We had some terrific guys," he said, "Wilber Marshall, Dave Duerson, Mike Singletary, Al Harris, Todd Bell. Those guys were all great, great players. It was too bad that Harris and Bell held out for better contracts and missed the Super Bowl season. That group gave us many opportunities. They truly did have a public swagger and identification. They were as good as any defense, probably in history, but our offense was designed to control the ball for 48 minutes out of 60, leaving our defense little time to get tired on the field."

The champions were not built overnight. As Ditka said, some guys were going to make it through his boot-camp practices, and some guys were going to be long gone by the time the Bears emerged as a serious league contender. Suhey is one player who was on the scene before Ditka took over, showed him he belonged, and participated in some of the greatest games and moments in Bears history.

"In 1981 and 1982, we had some seasoned players, but the team was basically transformed into a completely different team by Ditka," Suhey said. "The core of eight or 10 guys who were left were phenomenal together. Ditka turned it around. He said it was going to be a different team, and it was. It was a lot of fun. Looking back on it, we realized what we were going through, but it's easier to see now."

By 1986, after the Bears drafted Neal Anderson, Suhey's carries were diminishing. He didn't really complain, but said he hoped to remain a key fixture in the offense. Going gray as a young man, Suhey appeared older than he was, but he didn't want coaches and fans to think that meant he was nearing retirement. He said Ditka was thinking long-term, however.

"He wants a dynasty attitude on the Bears," Suhey said. "He wants it to be an attitude that's good for a number of years."

Suhey retired after the 1989 season, and at the end of his final home game at Soldier Field, his buddy Payton came onto the field in street clothes to walk him off.

"I leave with some reservations," said Suhey, who thought he could still play productively. "I wanted to leave the game at a certain level."

When Suhey's playing time dropped off as Anderson improved, he tried to be patient and avoid being looked at as a whiner. He said he had learned early in his career how important the team is.

"There's two rules in football," Suhey said. "Rule number one is, it's a team game. Rule number two is, you don't change rule number one."

Later in his career, Suhey had to wait his turn to resume his backfield partnership with Payton, but the friendship never waned. Within the team and the league, Payton was known as a practical joker who liked to have a good time. The casual fan wouldn't know this side of him, but Suhey was sometimes a participant, sometimes a victim.

"Oh yeah, he was a practical joker," Suhey said. "We had some good ones. I got picked on a few times, but we had some good ones together. I was right there with him."

The duo once took a hunting trip to Alaska together to see real Bears, teasing one another with the old joke about not having to run faster than the bears to survive a grizzly attack, only one another. None of those stories, however, are for public consumption in Suhey's mind—He prefers to talk about the magic Payton performed on the gridiron, with his speed, grace, creativity, and power while carrying the ball. When Payon died tragically young from liver disease at age 45 in 1999, some news reports related that Suhey was one of the few friends he saw near the end of his life.

"He was one of my closest friends," Suhey said.

For the men involved, Suhey-Payton was a partnership that transcended football, and their personalities and talents meshed perfectly—for the 1985 Bears and beyond.

14

GARY FENCIK

Gary Fenick played college football at Yale after growing up in the Chicago area, but his renaissance education on the musty campus environs in New Haven, Connecticut, didn't cure him of the passion he brought to clobbering guys. Not too many players from Ivy League schools earn graduate degrees in the National Football League, but Fenick acquired his second sheepskin with honors.

Cooperative, friendly with the media, and given to insightful answers, Fenick was a good guy off the field during his career with the Bears, but he was a terror on it. He was a secondary leader who always seemed to be in on the tackle, but who earned his popularity in a less flamboyant manner than some teammates. He did not lack for chutzpah, though, evidenced by his singing role on the 1985 Super Bowl-bound Bears' famous "The Super Bowl Shuffle."

John Gary Fenick was born June 11, 1954, in Chicago and attended high school in Barrington, a suburb of the Windy City. He played his college ball for the Bulldogs and in 1976 was drafted in the tenth round by the Miami Dolphins. By that fall, though, he was participating in 13 games for the Bears, beginning what would be his entire pro career—through the 1987 season—all in Chicago.

Fencik, who at 6-foot-1 and 194 pounds, appeared in 164 games for the Bears, retiring as the team's all-time tackler while intercepting 38 passes in his career. He was a super thief, a major league pickpocket who frustrated quarterbacks by ghosting through their line of vision to take away possible big gainers.

Fencik went through hard times with weak Bears teams, made himself valuable enough to keep during the rebuilding years, and then played a critical role on the Buddy Ryan defense during the glory years. So he saw it all with the Bears, from 6-10 regular seasons to playoff seasons that were rewards without the hope of advancing to the Super Bowl—to being part of the happy group that won it all.

That perspective of experiencing highs and lows, from a rookie in 1976 to being a member of the 1985 title team, affected Fencik's choice of the game of his life. The contest occurred during the run-up to the Super Bowl—a game that convinced Fencik that the Bears were better than they'd ever been during his time with the franchise.

November 17, 1985

TEXAS STADIUM
CHICAGO BEARS 44 - DALLAS COWBOYS 0
By Gary Fencik

It was my 10th year in the league, and we had never beaten the Cowboys—not in the preseason, regular season, or postseason. A win like that is part of the growing process.

First of all, it was meaningful because of what they had done and how they had earned the title of America's Team. That was a great franchise. Coach Ditka had played there, and Mike downplayed that, yet it had to be important to him. He had coached with Tom Landry, too. And Landry was still the coach. They had that America's team, kind of in-your-face attitude. That was an important notch to put on your belt. We beat them badly, and the defense recorded a shutout. No

Playing in the Bears' defensive backfield, Gary Fencik was also the last line of defense on the extraordinary Chicago defense of the 1985 Super Bowl era.
Photo by Jonathan Daniel/Getty Images

matter how good your defense is—and ours was very good—you rarely shut teams out. Nobody beat the Dallas Cowboys 44-0 in Dallas, but we beat them every way that day.

The defense had a swagger, and its reputation just grew all season with the success we had. We knew we had a good defense, but we had some adversity that year. Al Harris and Todd Bell were two regulars who held out for better contracts. There was always the hope that they would come back, and we would be even better. We would have been even more dominant than we were.

To be part of that was really fun.

The destruction of the Cowboys was a glimpse of what soon followed. A nation truly began to understand what a powerhouse the Bears were as they watched television that day. Observers of the Bears during the 1985 season and the 1986 playoffs never would say they lacked for confidence, but in the closing weeks of the season, as the playoffs beckoned, the team moved to a new level of near-perfect performance. New York Jets quarterback Joe Namath had already guaranteed a Super Bowl victory over the Baltimore Colts back when the National Football League-American Football League merger was fresh. The Bears matched Namath's brashness by creating "The Super Bowl Shuffle" video. Fencik was one of the eager participants, though he had no idea the video would become a smash hit.

"We certainly didn't think we would become video stars," he said, "or we probably wouldn't have done it. But you know, we had made the confirmation statements during the season about how good we were."

It's unlikely anyone was happier with the Bears' on-field stranglehold on the league that year than Fencik. He sensed he was approaching the end of his career, and he appreciated each joyful minute of the season. The Bears had completed the 1984 season with a 10-6 record and then had recorded another step of improvement by beating the Washington Redskins, 23-19, in the first round of the playoffs. But when Chicago lined up against the smooth, high-scoring San Franciso 49ers in the National Football Conference championship game, one could easily see that the Bears weren't ready for a prime-time assignment like the Super Bowl. The 49ers won 23-0.

Fencik was terribly disappointed and decided to get away from it all.

"I decided I was going to take a three-month trip to the Far East," he said. "I had never been there. So I went home after the game and pretty quickly thereafter bought a plane ticket that would allow me to travel in one direction. You couldn't backtrack. I started in Chicago and went to Tahiti."

His magical journey took him to Malaysia, Thailand, Hong Kong, China, the Philippines, and other countries.

"It was a great trip," Fencik said. "I thought about football very little. Well, I can't say very little because I was concerned about staying in shape. I was able to continue running, and I did a lot of isometrics. I was pretty confident when I got back to the United States that I could do whatever was needed to get back into football conditioning. That's why it was important to leave early, so that when I got back I would still have three or four months to get ready for the season."

There were lessons to be learned from watching the high-powered 49ers up close, too, and Fencik did not actually depart from the U.S. instantly after the Bears' abruptly ended 1984 season.

"That was certainly a crushing defeat," he said. "We had played really well in the first half and were down only 6-0 to the 49ers. But they clearly took control of the game in the second half. I actually went to the Super Bowl—it was played at Stanford that year—and it was pretty painful to watch that game knowing that we were basically one game away from being there ourselves. I was really kind of saying, 'You're going to have a very short time left to play and you want to play in one of these.'"

It was a Super Bowl Fencik could reach out and touch after a playoff game he could reflect upon with a couple of what-ifs. Most of all, he could envision that scenario turning out differently the next season.

"I absolutely thought the team was still on the rise," he said. "And there's no question there was promise for the next year. I was ready to be part of doing something special. It's kind of odd. You definitely have both feet in and you're really going to commit yourself to have a great year. On the other hand, you're looking at that hourglass, and it certainly isn't getting extended. There were some things I wanted to do in the off-season, and the trip to the Far East was at the top of my list."

Fencik said his memory isn't clear about just how much confidence the Bears had going into the 1985 season, but that defeating Washington in the playoffs was a stick-to-the-ribs victory.

"It was, 'Okay, we really do have a good team,'" Fencik said. "We really controlled Washington, particularly in the fourth quarter. That was a good team, and it gave us a lot of confidence. I think you have to win in the playoffs in order to really believe that you've earned the right to get to the next step.

"Earlier in my career, we got to the playoffs a couple of times, a wild-card berth, and we lost," he said. "You might think you've accomplished something, but I think you really need to win. If you win in the playoffs, then you know you're making progress."

The Bears continued to improve through the 1985 season. The Dallas game was a milestone, but the team peaked for the playoffs. Most people remember the 46-10 trouncing of the New England Patriots for the Bears' title. Fewer remember that the Bears were perhaps more dominating in the two playoff games leading up to the Super Bowl. The Bears took out the New York Giants 21-0 in the first round and wiped out the Los Angeles Rams, 24-0, in the NFC championship game.

Fencik, who is a partner in a money management firm in Chicago and still resides in the area, not long ago had a friend in his office talking about the Super Bowl team. The other two victories were just dim memories for him.

"I think people forget what the score was in the two previous games, that we shut out two teams in the playoffs," Fencik said. "I mean, that's pretty impressive stuff."

Despite the defense's wild personalities and terrific achievements, Fencik won't minimize the offense's contributions.

"It wasn't like we were just a small-time offense," Fencik said. "We had Walter Payton. We had a lot of speed at wide out. We had a super offensive line.

"I know there was always some criticism about Willie Gault's catching ability, but he averaged 21.3 yards per catch. The key statistic for quarterbacks and for indicators of success in the NFL is yards-per-pass attempts, and I think Jim McMahon was right at the top that year. Willie really stretched the defense so much. I saw it in practice. He just had so much speed that he would go deep in the secondary and allow deep gaps to open up underneath."

Fencik admired Payton's toughness as a runner. Defenders make their livings putting backs on the ground, knocking the stuffing out of them with hard hits, and Fencik was glad Payton was on his side. Sometimes Payton acted as if he wanted to get even with defenders as much as he wanted to make yardage.

"Walter had that ability to deliver a blow," Fencik said. "He got kind of a stalemate and kept on running. It's that second effort that you see time and time again on highlight films with him. But you know when you actually have to make contact with him he's going to pop you."

Fencik has remained in the area where he grew up, and he still follows up close the team he played for—he's a season ticket holder. One of the highlights—both as a fan and player—has always been the intense rivalry between the Bears and the Green Bay Packers.

"You know, with the tradition between the Bears and Packers the games certainly have historical significance," Fencik said. "I think it was important when Lovie Smith took over as coach that he said it was a goal to beat the Packers. I think you have to beat whomever you have to in order to get to the Super Bowl. But I know what he meant."

15

EMERY MOOREHEAD

When you play tight end for a coach who practically invented the modern version of the position, you know you are going to hear about every accomplishment and every mistake. Emery Moorehead was the Bears' Super Bowl tight end, and he found playing for Mike Ditka to be a continuing education course. Moorehead felt his coach took a very active interest in whatever the tight end was doing on the field. After all, who would know better?

"Number one," Moorehead said, "the very first play he looked at when he looked at film was the tight end. It was, 'What is this guy doing?' I wasn't the big bruiser he was—I played at 228 pounds in the Super Bowl—but he had a lot of respect for me, and he always tells me, 'You know, you did a helluva job for me.'"

Moorehead said being a tight end in the National Football League was one of the most demanding roles that could be filled. If Ditka (who wasn't that much bigger than Moorehead) enhanced the profile of the position when he played, the view has shifted again over the years. Once upon a time, the tight end was primarily a blocker. Then the role expanded to encompass more pass catching, though the blocking responsibility remained crucial. Now pass catching has become more important than blocking for tight ends—at least that's the way Moorehead looks at things.

"Football has become so specialized that you've got two-down players," he said. "They claim one guy can't block so he comes out in pass protection. They put in ones that can catch with wide receivers. In the 1980s, when I played, they were beginning to use the tight end, placing more emphasis on playing the all-around position. It usually worked out that the tight end saw more balls from the quarterback when he had a good running back. I had Walter Payton. When you've got somebody who can run the football like that, you can get the most out of the tight end down field.

"Not only did Walter make my job blocking easy, but the fact that the linebackers and everybody else on defense had to respect Walter's running ability really set up the play-action for me. Of course, Jim McMahon, our quarterback, was a huge fan of the tight end when he played for Brigham Young University. I think his tight end at BYU caught about 80 passes. Jim started with the Bears in 1982, and I started in 1981. I don't know if I caught every pass in my career from Jim, but I caught quite a few. He helped me.

"A guy like Payton lets you do so many things," Moorehead continued. "It made the job easier for everybody, having a guy like that on your team. Defenses keyed on him all of the time, and others like me got open."

As a versatile tight end, Moorehead played a part in the running game as a blocker and in the passing game as a receiver. Everyone knew the Bears were going to establish the run first, but sometimes they were caught off-guard via the air.

"Mike Ditka was a guy who made sure we knew we were going to run the football," Moorehead said. "We were going to run the football no matter what. The defense could put nine guys up on the line, 10 guys, it didn't matter. We were going to run the football because we had the greatest running back in football. Not just the greatest running back, but the greatest football player of all time. I mean

The regular Bears' tight end during the Super Bowl era was Emery Moorehead, who enjoyed the task of playing for a coach who virtually invented the modern tight end position. *Photo by Jonathan Daniel/Getty Images*

Walter even threw like 11 touchdown passes in his career. I know he's way up there on the list of all-time Bears pass receivers, too. You're talking about a helluva football player."

Indeed, what inspired even more respect from many Bears coaches and players was the fact that a superstar like Payton never hesitated to throw his body into danger zones by blocking for teammates.

"He made a heck of a block on plays," Moorehead said. "In the game we played in 1985 against Minnesota, when McMahon came off the bench and threw for three touchdowns, Walter made a helluva block on a linebacker and saved the play. The guy was getting ready to kill McMahon. Walter hit him right in the knees and sent him right over the top of him, allowing McMahon to hit Dennis McKinnon with a touchdown. The guy was a complete football player. You don't see that anymore."

Emery Matthew Moorehead was born March 22, 1954, in Evanston, Illinois, and grew up there, just north of Chicago, where he became a fan of the Chicago Cubs and Ernie Banks. He played college football at the University of Colorado and was a sixth-round draft choice of the New York Giants in 1977. Moorehead spent three years with the Giants and one year with the Denver Broncos before playing the final eight years of his career with the Bears. The move to the Bears was extremely exciting for a homegrown talent like Moorehead who as a youth rooted for the Bears of the Gale Sayers and Dick Butkus era.

"It was awfully important to me [to return to Chicago]," Moorehead said. "Number one because I grew up a Bears fan, and so to get a chance to play for your home team was very special. But to win it all, I understood how long it had been and how frustrating it had been. You know I understood that if you won a Super Bowl here in Chicago, you were in here forever. You were in for life."

The Bears who came within one game of advancing to the Super Bowl in 1984, but fell to San Francisco, left the scene of the crime absolutely knowing they would be back and would go farther the next season. Ditka even told the players, Moorehead recalled.

"Everybody came back with a purpose," he said.

In Moorehead's mind, the games of his life were games from the 1985 season that were critical markers, games that gave the Bears important momentum towards the Super Bowl championship.

September 8, 1985

SOLDIER FIELD
CHICAGO BEARS 38 - TAMPA BAY BUCCANEERS 28
By Emery Moorehead

The very first game was against Tampa Bay. We had the best defense in the league in 1984, but in the new season, we fell behind and gave up a lot of points right away. We gave up 28 points in the first half. Everybody was a little bit confused.

At halftime, things were tense, but we regrouped. Then cornerback Leslie Frazier made a great interception and returned it for a touchdown. That got the ball rolling, and we overcame it. Our defense shut them out in the second half.

We could have dug ourselves a hole at the beginning of the season. It's so important to get off to a good start. We could have blown it right there in the first game, but then the offense came back and scored.

In the second Tampa Bay game that season a month later in Tampa when we won 27-19, we were down at the half again. I made a lot of big plays in that game, and we scored late in the game. That was the only 100-yard receiving game I had in my career.

***

Moorehead was 6-foot-2 and played at as little as 217 pounds, according to pro football record books. But by his own account, he weighed as much as 20 pounds more at times as well. He dabbled at running back with the Giants, but saw little serious action until after he joined the Bears in 1981. Beginning in 1982, Moorehead had a nice stretch of receiving for the Bears with seasonal catch totals of 30, 42, 29, and 35 receptions. Those were his finest seasons in a career that ended in 1988. Moorehead retired to live in the Chicago suburbs, works in real estate, owns a construction services company, and remains active in Bears alumni affairs. His son Aaron plays for the Indianapolis Colts.

For his career, Moorehead hauled in 224 passes for an average per catch of 13.3 yards, an impressive number for a tight end who spent much of his career as a safety valve second or third option for a quarterback. One of the extraordinary things about that Bears team that posted 456 total points was that 21 players scored. From leading scorer Kevin Butler, the kicker, to defensive lineman Steve McMichael, who notched a safety, nearly half the members of the team put up points. Likewise, 14 different players caught passes. Moorehead's 35 catches were second only to Payton, who had 49.

"Walter led us in catches that year," Moorehead said. "Dennis McKinnon had a ton of touchdowns [seven]. Willie Gault was great on the deep passes and kickoffs. Matt Suhey had a lot of catches. Everybody contributed. That's the thing about playing on a great team. You see everybody step up and play. Butler was a rookie and he kicked 51 out of 51 extra points on touchdowns. That's a lot of touchdowns. When you started getting the ball at the 50-yard line, then all you needed was 15 yards, and you were in Butler's range. He was young and strong. Everything was working that year as a team. That really was what got us there, the team effort."

During the course of even the best seasons by superior teams, certain games are in jeopardy of being lost, but are reversed. One of Moorehead's best game memories from that season occurred when the Bears won one that looked like it was slipping away. Chicago was trying to establish its dominance early in the season. The Thursday night game carried a national television audience and played a huge role in establishing the Jim McMahon leadership legend.

Under no circumstances, Ditka vowed, would the injured McMahon get into the game. Ditka feared his quarterback might be sidelined for the season if he got hit wrong.

The Vikings were also a hot team, starting 2-0, and they took a 17-9 halftime lead. McMahon would wander past Ditka and casually inform him he could play if needed. He threw warmup passes and said, "Put me in, Coach." He dropped hints on the sideline that he was ready, nagging Ditka and driving him buggy. Finally, halfway through the third quarter, Ditka relented, inserting McMahon.

September 19, 1985

HUBERT H. HUMPHREY METRODOME
CHICAGO BEARS 33 - MINNESOTA VIKINGS 24
By Emery Moorehead

We were down and McMahon was hurt. He came off the bench. He was begging Ditka to let him in, let him in, let him in. But he hadn't practiced all week. Ditka had a rule: if you don't practice, you're not going to play. McMahon was running around, though, tugging on his (Ditka's) shirt. Finally, he put him in.

Then, on the first play he and Willie had that long touchdown. Then there was an interception and a turnover; and we got the ball back. The very first play after that McMahon hit Dennis McKinnon for another touchdown—all on national television.

Our defense got another turnover, and McMahon hit McKinnon again for another touchdown. It was like three out of four passes, or four out of five passes going for touchdowns, and we came back to win. That win really put us on the map. Everybody saw it, and everybody said, "Well, these guys are for real, man. They've got an offense to go with this defense."

***

Despite that explosion and despite being part of a unit that featured Walter Payton and scored points by the bushel, Moorehead knows that the defense's swagger and image still pervade in the minds of fans of that Super Bowl team.

"Defense is part of the Chicago image. You get a good defense, and the town is happy, man, because they can always brag, 'We've got a great defense' that just knocks the other team out. When you get a defense together, the offense comes along. In our case, the 'D' provided so many turnovers that year and scored so many points. You usually think the offense will get the ball on the 20-yard line, and it's got to go 80 yards. But when you start getting the ball on the plus side of the 50-yard line, the scoring percentages go up tremendously."

The Bears who won the 1986 Super Bowl by cruising through the playoffs had as many colorful actors on the big stage as *The Producers*—fun-loving personalities like McMahon, Ditka, and the newly introduced William "Refrigerator" Perry entertained the masses that season.

"[Perry] just loved to play football," Moorehead said. "He was young and enthusiastic and Ditka put him on offense because our defensive coordinator, Buddy Ryan, wouldn't play him on defense. So that's how we ended up with a 300-pound running back going for first downs and in our goal-line offense. He was a great personality, too, and The Fridge had his own cheerleaders, the Fridgerettes. Everybody wanted to talk to The Fridge."

Moorehead said the most amazing thing about the whole experience is how quickly time has passed since the championship. At the time he spoke, all sorts of plans were being made for 20-year reunion events.

"Everybody wants McMahon or The Fridge," Moorehead chuckled. "McMahon took a lot of heat for us being the personality he was. He put a lot of pressure on himself. Time just flies, you know? When the Bears won the title in 1963 they couldn't believe that 17 years had passed since the club last won it, and when we won it, 22 years had passed. Now we're looking at the same type of situation. You're talking about generations of kids who have no idea who the 1985 Bears and Walter Payton are. I was at an engagement, and I said, 'You know Dan Marino is going into the Hall of Fame,' and they're like, 'Who's Dan Marino?'"

The Bears have won championships dating back to the earliest days of the NFL in the 1920s, but they have won just one Super Bowl title. Given the additional passage of time between Bears successes, that winning team imprinted its achievement on the city for all time's sake.

"There's something about the first, you know," Moorehead said. "When you are part of the first, it's something special."

16

KEVIN BUTLER

The easy-going kicker with a flair for having a good time shared a relationship with the short-tempered coach with a penchant for screaming his lungs out that probably wouldn't last if they were headed down the aisle. Somehow, though, the diametrically opposite personalities of place kicker Kevin Butler and Mike Ditka never interfered with results.

Butler, a terrific kicker for the Bears, placated the boss' nerves with his successful boots just enough to prevent Ditka from strangling him. Of course, Ditka had a funny way of showing his faith in his kicker, yelling at Butler, berating him, never offering choice ego-boosting compliments when a fiery obscenity would do.

"I guess he was very moody when it came to kickers," said Butler, who won the job as a rookie in 1985, the Bears' Super Bowl season. "I guess if Prozac would have been prevalent in 1985, I probably would have been on it. I think his fuse was even shorter with punters. We went through several punters during my career with the Bears. Mike was tough with me, but Mike also knew that I responded to that. I didn't shy away from him getting in my face. You know there were times I would go out on the field, and his last words to me would be, 'You're the worst f-----g kicker I've ever seen!' And, you know, you're walking out there, and you're going to kick. I got some kind of confidence out of that statement."

During a September 14, 1986, home game against the Philadelphia Eagles, Ditka dissed him, and Butler was starting to agree. The game went into overtime tied at 10-10, primarily because Butler had succeeded on just one of five field-goal attempts.

"It was an off day," Butler said. "I was hitting good field-goal kicks, but the wind was knocking them down short. I think my last kick in regulation was from 55 yards, and I really thought I just nailed it. It was right down the barrel, but into a little bit of wind, and it fell three or four yards short. I think I hit the upright on another kick. So it was one of those days when nobody in the world liked the kicker— and the kicker didn't even like the kicker. I was at the point where we had fourth down and three yards to go for a first down, and I was looking at Ditka and saying, 'I think we should go for it today, Coach.'"

The Bears kicked off to start the overtime period against the Eagles, and Butler wondered if it might be the last kickoff of his career.

"Because if the Bears had lost the game, I couldn't have blamed Mike if he did get rid of me," Butler said. "It was one of those games. But I think Mike also understood that some days you have tough games, and you know you just have to persevere and try to get through it."

What rescued Butler—his psyche, at least—is that he had a bad day, and the Bears still won.

"We kicked off; they fumbled the kickoff, and we got a first down," Butler said. "We ran it. I think when Ed Hughes [the offensive coordinator] thought we'd kick a field goal, Ditka would look at me and go, 'Hell no, run it again.' We ran and got another yard. Hughes said, 'Let's kick it now.' Ditka said, 'The kid can't make anything.' We got to third down. Do we kick now? No. Fourth down. Now Ditka is

Kicker Kevin Butler was a rookie when the Bears won the Super Bowl after the 1985 season. He and coach Mike Ditka had some interesting confrontations, but Butler said he thrived on the challenge, and they remain close today.
Photo by Jonathan Daniel/Getty Images

looking at me like, 'You are the worst kicker ever.' He looked me up and down and said, 'Just try to go out there and put your foot on the ball. I'm not even gonna watch.'

"Those were his exact last words when I ran out on the field. I kick the field goal. I make it. We win 13-10. I come back over to him, and go, 'Hey, Coach, I told you I'd make it.' He looked me square in the eyes with his hard look, and said, 'And I told you I wasn't going to watch.' I was like, 'Okay, I totally understand where you're coming from.'"

Kevin Gregory Butler was born July 24, 1962, in Savannah, Georgia. He had good size for a kicker, standing six feet tall and weighing 215 pounds—and he was no latecomer to booting extra points and field goals. He was a star at Redan High School in Stone Mountain, Georgia, and at the University of Georgia. Butler earned enough notoriety to be drafted with the Bears' No. 4 pick in 1985— a strong testimony to his strong leg, since most kickers find their way onto rosters through the free-agent route.

Butler did not rattle easily, and despite tremendous productivity with the Bears—with whom he played between 1985 and 1995 before wrapping up his NFL career with two seasons in Arizona—some of his favorite kicks were made before he ever saw Chicago. His foot was the most valuable appendage in the Georgia AAA State Championship when he kicked a field goal for Redan that provided the winning margin in a 17-14 victory over Marist High.

In college, Butler booted a 60-yard, game-ending field goal to give his Bulldogs a win over rival Clemson. The Bears knew what kind of leg they were drafting. The 1985 Bears were poised to storm the pro football world with an experienced club that had paid its dues and matured together. But they often relied on a 23-year-old rookie all season to make the difference.

Butler had an extraordinary debut season, shrugging off pressure, doing exactly what the Bears asked of him, never faltering in key situations. Butler made 51 of 51 points after touchdowns while threading an aforementioned 31 of 37 field-goal attempts (83.8

percent). In all, he scored a team-leading 144 points. A championship contender cannot putter around with a weak link at kicker. Butler took the worry out of the position for the veterans.

When the Super Bowl rolled around, the team knew it could count on Butler. It's probably a good thing, however, that the coaches and his teammates didn't know what was going through his mind when Super Bowl Sunday arrived in New Orleans.

January 26, 1986

THE SUPERDOME
CHICAGO BEARS 46 - NEW ENGLAND PATRIOTS 10
By Kevin Butler

I had a big Super Bowl with three field goals [28, 24, and 24 yards] and five extra points. I remember it all. I especially remember coming out on the field and thinking we had a chance for a third field goal right before halftime. I already had two, but my previous experiences in the Superdome had not gone well. I had played there in the Sugar Bowl two out of my four years in college for national championships, and we didn't win either one of them. We played against Pittsburgh and Penn State.

You go into the stadium a little superstitious, as kickers are. I didn't really want to tell anybody about those experiences, so I didn't. I kept my mouth shut because I didn't want to jinx myself.

Going into the game against the Patriots, we felt if we did not turn the ball over, we would win. It was a very confident team. I think we were confident because of the success we had, and that confidence became the overall demeanor of that team. Then, on the first play of the game, Walter Payton fumbled. The Patriots scored on a field goal, and all of a sudden, we all looked at each other like, "Oh no, here it goes. This is what we can't do."

At that point, we got a chance to kick a field goal and kind of get ourselves back into the game. My heart was pumping out of my shoulder pads—which really weren't shoulder pads—but I could feel my heart. It was very intense, much more intense in that game for it to stick out in my mind. Making every kick in the Super Bowl was very important.

When we got up 23-3, we were having a little bit more fun. You're relaxed. You're staring a world championship right in the eye in the third quarter. It was very exciting. You know, the extra points, the kick-off, just being out on the field and knowing what we accomplished was something I'll never forget.

***

The Super Bowl triumph was the biggest win Butler experienced in his 11 seasons with the Bears—five of which concluded with more than 100 points scored. But the most tension-packed kick Butler made in his Bears career occurred during a regular-season game. He was one Bear who appreciated the significance of the rivalry with the Green Bay Packers that dated back to the 1920s. And Butler was one Bear who got the chance to face down the Packers with the game on the line. No wonder it remains a wonderful memory.

November 8, 1987

LAMBEAU FIELD
CHICAGO BEARS 26 - GREEN BAY PACKERS 24
By Kevin Butler

It was a helluva ballgame, back and forth. Al Del Greco kicked a field goal for them with a minute or two left that put the Packers up. It looked as if it would be the first time the Packers beat us since we won the Super Bowl. The place was going crazy. I remember Jim McMahon, our quarterback coming over to me and saying, "Get ready. I'll get you in position. Just get ready."

They hadn't even kicked off yet. We were looking at possibly going the length of the field without any time, when McMahon said, 'We're gonna get you up there, and you're gonna have a chance.' I was thinking that I wouldn't want to do it to anyone more than the

Packers. We ran a few plays and got a long pass play to work. There were about four seconds left in the game, and we went out there and lined up for a 52-yard field goal.

The field was chewed up and muddy, just classic conditions for a Bears-Packers game at Lambeau. It was a little bit cool, rainy, and it had been overcast the whole game. Just as I started to kick the field goal, the Packers called time out. They wanted to ice me and make me nervous, but actually they allowed me and Mike Tomczak, our backup quarterback and my holder, to flatten out the kicking surface. It was the 42-yard line, pretty much midfield, so it was really chewed up. That one time out probably cost the Packers a game. They gave me time to stamp out my foot plan and get a nice spot for Mike to put the ball down. That really enabled me to make the kick.

The play really backfired on the Packers; and when that ball sailed through the uprights, you could have heard a piece of cheese drop in Wisconsin. Tomczak lifted me up in the air. The team ran out on the field, and it was just a euphoric time. Although I was a kicker, I was really a football player at heart. A rivalry like Bears-Packers brought out the best in me. I knew it brought out the best in my teammates, too. When you get in games like that, and you actually make a play to decide a game, that sticks with you.

The Packers kick would be the one moment that I think helped define me with the fans of Chicago. To be honest, I think they liked me and my personality the first couple of years I was there; but if you can put the dagger in the heart of the Packers, I think you gain a spot in every Bears fan's heart.

It was a good thing that Butler comprehended Ditka's ways or he might have had a nervous breakdown. He didn't let the head man discourage him when periodically Ditka reverted and blasted him. During a game against Tampa Bay, at a different point in his Bears career, Butler and Ditka had a brief verbal showdown.

"It was another time he told me I was a lousy kicker," Butler said. "I looked back at him and said, 'Well, if you think you can get someone better, get someone better.'

"A couple of days later at practice, Ditka stopped the drills in order to take field-goal practice. He ordered the kicking squad onto the field. When Butler ran out to take his place, Ditka yelled, "Butler! Get out of there!"

"I step out, and this kid I've never seen before steps in," Butler said. "He's a barefooted kicker, and Ditka went out and saw him that morning. This kid stood up there and kicked about four field goals. The first one almost hit the linemen. The second one went right. The third one went left. He missed all of them. Ditka blew the whistle and shouted, 'Offense. Defense.'

"I figured I was fired again. As the players switched, he yelled, 'Butler! Get over here!' I go over to him and say, 'Yes, sir.' He goes, "Don't you ever f-----g challenge me again.' I went, 'Yes, sir, I understand.'

"It was his way of communicating. I always felt like I was Ditka's kicker. Through all the turmoil, all the stuff, that was very critical—whether he was on my ass, or whether he was talking me up like he always did. I mean he would say things to me, but when it came time to talk to the newspaper, I never heard him say that he didn't believe in me. As a kicker, the confidence of your coach would be the most critical thing you could lose.

"When the coach loses confidence, the next thing that happens is that the players lose confidence. I think a lot of kickers go through that problem nowadays. Sensitive would be a crazy word to use for Mike, but I think he was sensitive to that awareness. He could challenge me. I was different from a lot of kickers. I know kickers a lot better than me who could not have lasted one year under Mike Ditka because they don't like confrontations, they don't like being challenged, or challenged in front of people. I think, when the Bears drafted me, they knew what my psyche was and how I approached the game, so it was no problem for me. He really helped me be a better kicker."

However, Butler realized one other important facet of place kicking. You can have the best leg in the gridiron universe, but you aren't going to succeed at the job unless you have some help once the ball is hiked.

"You're only as good as your holder," Butler said.

These days, Butler is vice president of Experiential Marketing Company, and lives in the Atlanta suburbs. The firm helps large companies with their branding, their communication programs, and dealer meetings. The company is a global venture, and he travels frequently. Often, Butler returns to Chicago on business, where the firm has an office downtown on Michigan Avenue.

Butler said he is still recognized regularly on those visits, particularly when eating at Gibson's, a popular steak house, which is a favorite of his.

"They treat you like gold," he said of the restaurant. "It's amazing how the people come up to me. They treat me wonderfully at Ditka's restaurant, too. I spend a lot of time in Ditka's. I take a lot of people there. When Coach is there, he'll be the first guy to come over, and he'll say, 'This is the worst f-----g kicker I ever had' to my friends. He does it endearingly. He is a dear friend, and he is a very loyal, loyal, loyal person. I think everybody in Chicago certainly realizes that."

17

TOM THAYER

He was a Bears fan growing up. He was a Bear during his playing days. And now that Tom Thayer is retired, he is still involved with the Bears. He was a Chicago-area guy all of the way and still is.

Thayer, a guard on the Bears' 1985 Super Bowl team, grew up in Joliet, Illinois, about 50 miles south of Chicago, and he played high school ball at Joliet Catholic. Then he attended Notre Dame, about 100 miles east of Chicago. Thayer was a 1983 fourth-round draft pick of the Bears but played with the Chicago Blitz and Arizona Wranglers of the United States Football League before joining the NFL club. Thayer signed his USFL contract before learning he had been taken by the Bears, and at first wondered if he had squandered the opportunity to make his dream come true. But he made up for it as part of the Bears during some of the most glorious years of the franchise.

In high school, Thayer was a terrific all-around athlete. Besides lettering four years as a lineman in football, he was also a wrestler and track man, setting a school record of 51 feet for throwing the shot. Over the years he maintained ties with Joliet, attending home football games and operating a deli with family members—including his older brother Rick, whom he cites as an inspirational influence on his football career. Reminiscing about 10 years ago, Thayer's high school football coach, Gene Gillespie, was quoted as saying Thayer "… played every down like it was the Super Bowl."

Thayer was an All-American at Notre Dame, winning four letters playing under Dan Devine and Gerry Faust. Thayer played on a Fighting Irish team that went up against Herschel Walker's Georgia team for the national championship.

Thayer, who is 6-foot-4 and weighed 280 pounds during his pro playing days, was given credit in the team's 1986 media guide for a 500-pound bench press. The information book proclaimed him "… strongest member of Bear squad."

Thomas Allen Thayer was born August 16, 1961, and spent eight of his nine National Football League seasons with the Bears. His final 1993 season was spent with the Miami Dolphins. With his background in the USFL, Thayer was a more seasoned rookie than most when he finally hooked up with the Bears. When the 1985 season began, he was a member of a veteran squad that had grand aspirations and thought it had the capability of being a Super Bowl contender. However, Thayer began that season on the bench as a backup.

When Thayer thinks back on his career and that inaugural season he focuses on an early-season game that had special meaning for most Bears because it was a come-from-behind victory; but Thayer selected this game for two more personal reasons.

September 19, 1985

HUBERT H. HUMPHREY METRODOME
CHICAGO BEARS 33 - MINNESOTA VIKINGS 24
By Tom Thayer

Personally, that was a doubly memorable game. We won, I got into the game, and I started from that point on. The first two weeks of the season I did nothing. I just sat around. I maybe played on a kickoff return.

Tom Thayer, a nine-year Bear, including the Super Bowl year, is from Joliet in the Chicago area, and maintains close ties to the team and area today with his in-season broadcasting duties. *Photo by Jonathan Daniel/Getty Images*

This was the game that Jim McMahon came in at quarterback and threw all of the touchdowns. He wasn't supposed to play because of an injury, but he came into the game after begging Coach Ditka on the sideline to let him play. The Bears were doing well then, and we had a Monday night edition of the NFL on Thursday night.

We were getting beat pretty good by Minnesota. McMahon hadn't participated in any drills. Finally, Ditka put him in the game, and the end result of the first play was a touchdown pass. It was a play he kind of improvised. It was supposed to be a screen. Walter Payton had an unbelievable blitz pickup. He just crushed the guy with a block, and McMahon threw a touchdown pass to Willie Gault.

It gave the team a feeling of relief. We were down by two and a half touchdowns, and all of a sudden, we got a different feeling. We scored again right after that, and it just changed the whole profile for everybody—those playing in the game and everyone in the stadium.

I started the game on the bench again, but the guy playing in front of me got injured. I went in and started playing and did okay pretty much from my first play. From that moment on, I played and continued to play right on through the Super Bowl. The injury gave me an opportunity to take advantage at that point. Just because I went into the game didn't mean that I was guaranteed to stay in there. In pro sports, if you get an opportunity presented to you, you play.

I felt pretty good after the game. I was glad we won, but the coaches didn't say anything special to me afterwards. As an offensive lineman, no matter how many snaps you play, or no matter what you do, you know you never walked out of the stadium patting yourself on the back or having the coaches pat you on the back. I'm not sure if they noticed anything. They didn't give me any feedback then.

But once you leave the stadium and you start watching the game on tape, it's different. The coaches talk then. You start being coached as a player who's going to be in there. The coaching evaluation is much stricter.

We kept on winning, and I played every game. It was a confident football team. Everybody pretty much figured out we were going to win if we continued to work hard. It's not that we became overconfident, or became complacent, or tried to walk through it. We just figured out that, if we kept playing at the same high level at which we were playing, we could do it because we were a good football team.

***

Thayer's Bears beginnings sound like a Hollywood movie plot. He gets a break to play because of injury, the team is trailing and comes back to win, and he keeps the job all the way through the run to the title.

Hold up the championship trophy and fade to black.

Being an offensive guard is one of the most anonymous roles in football, and on the 1985 team, the defense overshadowed the offense.

"Anytime anybody talks about the 1985 Bears, they talk about the defensive part of the ball," Thayer said. "But the offense contributed pretty heavily. The offense allowed the defense to be successful in many ways because you know we controlled the ball for over 36 minutes a game—and we scored points. You talk about an hour-long football game, if your offense is controlling the ball for more than 30 minutes a game, and there's another four minutes for special teams, that means there's only about 20 minutes a game that the defense has got to go out there and beat their ass."

Thayer, who said he bought 20 tickets a game for friends and relatives and could have used 50, believes that the Bears offense was underrated if only for one reason—Walter Payton, the fabulous running back was The Man.

"It was unbelievable for me blocking for Walter, because I grew up in the area as a kid," Thayer said. "For me, the whole Walter deal was different. I was in the eighth grade when the Bears drafted Walter Payton. Walter Payton was a hero to me at that point. Then I went to Notre Dame, and being a football fan, I was watching Walter get bigger and bigger. Then I went to the Bears, and I stood in the same huddle with him. The whole experience of growing into an opportunity to play with Walter Payton was unbelievable."

Thayer considered it a thrill just to be one of the lineman who helped open holes for Payton as he piled up rushing yards by the thousands.

"Walter was such a stud, and he was so respected," Thayer said, "you just understood who you were blocking for. It's amazing what he was capable of doing, what he did, and the effort he gave as a running back. Imagine being a kid growing up and watching him and wanting to be a football player your whole life and then all of a sudden running over a hill at training camp with Walter Payton and standing in a huddle with him. For me, it was just so amazing. It's just hard for non-football people to understand."

Being a local boy made good with the Bears, having a lifetime background of watching the team, Thayer also could appreciate the rivalry with the Green Bay Packers better than most.

"Everybody knows what beating Green Bay is all about," he said. "I grew up with that my whole life. But you know what? I kind of came along in an era where it was expected we would beat Green Bay. I came in during an era where we were kicking butt, and Green Bay wasn't as good. This more recent stretch with the Packers winning all of the time with Brett Favre kills me.

"Coach Ditka talked about it a lot. But with him we had to win every game, and that's the way he preached it. It wasn't just get jacked up for the Packers games, or division games—it's every game. But he understood controlling the division is the way you control your destiny, so he was a big advocate of winning every one of those games. At the time, it seemed like Minnesota was a better football team than Green Bay; so that was a real emotional game, too. The way he motivated us was to make it appear that we would lose our jobs if we played poorly. That's always true, but Ditka had a way of making it a little bit more serious."

The infamous Ditka glower—his ability to seemingly look right through players when he got angry—was always memorable. He often backed up his growl with a bite as well.

"I think every coach tries to motivate by fear of having players think they'll lose their job," Thayer said. "All of them have standards. But can they look players in the eye and make it stick? You know, all coaches tell you that they have expectations of you. Ditka was a great player. He was an assistant coach and then the head coach. When he's telling you to play better or else, he's got a little bit more credibility."

Thayer still lives in Chicago, and when he is not surfing in Hawaii, he follows the Bears very closely—as a member of the team's broadcasting crew covering the games. He said he often watches *Monday Night Football* with other members of the Super Bowl team such as offensive linemen Jay Hilgenberg and Keith Van Horne; and he plays racquetball with Jim McMahon.

During the 2005 preseason, when most pundits were picking the Bears to win a maximum of six to eight games, Thayer saw past the negative analysis and said he saw tremendous potential. He spotted young talent at most positions and guys with limited experience coming along.

"I think they could be a helluva team," he said.

Thayer was absolutely right. The Bears of 2005 fooled almost all of the experts and recorded their best season in years.

18

MIKE SINGLETARY

His nickname was "Samurai", and Mike Singletary was a warrior on the football field. The violence that poured out of him on the gridiron, pounding opposing ball carriers, seemed to be a contradictory aspect of his personality. Off the field, Singletary was a deeply religious, well-spoken, mature individual, who provided thoughtful answers to questions.

That persona co-existed, however, with the heart of a rugged football player who had no compunctions about roughing up the other team. Singletary was single-minded on the football field, a defender who wreaked havoc so efficiently that he was repeatedly selected as an all-star linebacker, leading to his 1998 induction into the Pro Football Hall of Fame in Canton, Ohio.

Michael Singletary was born October 9, 1958, in Houston, Texas, and played college football at Baylor University, where he became an All-American and a two-time Southwest Conference player of the year. After averaging 15 tackles a game, Singletary was chosen as a member of the conference's all-1970s team—while still a player. He actually recorded a stupefying 30 or more tackles in a game three times in college, with a high of 33.

Singletary was a second-round draft pick of the Bears in 1981 and spent his entire NFL career with Chicago. Singletary played 179 games for the Bears between 1981 and 1992 as a 6-foot, 230-pound linebacker. While his singing and dancing are not generally mentioned amongst his credentials, Singletary was one of the co-conspirators who participated in the 1985 Bears' "The Super Bowl Shuffle" video that became a huge hit.

Years before Singletary's arrival, the Bears had established a reputation for attracting and featuring great middle linebackers. He was preceded by the late Bill George, the great Dick Butkus, and followed by all-star Brian Urlacher.

"It is a special thing to be a linebacker with the Bears," Singletary said. "I don't know if there is another position so identified with a team. That's the truth. Coming to Chicago, I was really, really excited and happy to know I had to live up to something. Defense meant something, and playing middle linebacker meant something. That was very exciting to me."

Articulate and reflective about the role and responsibility of a professional athlete in society, Singletary penned an autobiography *Singletary on Singletary* with Jerry Jenkins in 1991. He also wrote books on family life, and in 2005 released a book called *Singletary: One-on-One*, written with Jay Carty.

As Singletary aged into his 40s, he took steps to begin an NFL coaching career, first as an assistant coach with the Baltimore Ravens, and then with the San Francisco 49ers. His dream is to one day become a pro head coach and perhaps even lead the Bears from the sidelines with the same vigor he did on the field.

Singletary had hoped to catch on with the Bears as an assistant coach in the early 2000s, but it didn't happen. When Singletary joined the Ravens for the 2003 season, he proclaimed that he would always be a Bear at heart, but that he was doing a job now working for another team and trying to help it stay a winner. He said he was thankful the Ravens gave him a chance.

Feared linebacker Mike Singletary—nicknamed Samurai—became a Hall of Fame defender with the Bears. He is now an assistant coach for the San Francisco 49ers and hopes to someday be an NFL head coach. *Photo by Jonathan Daniel/Getty Images*

From the beginning, Singletary said that he would be a coach who taught not only football, but character and respect for the sport, other players, and teammates. Singletary is one pro athlete who still believes that high-profile football, basketball, and baseball players—for that matter, athletes in all sports—can be role models for youngsters.

"There are a lot of guys out there doing a great job," Singletary said. "And a lot women are doing a great job, too. It just comes down to those who are willing to accept the responsibility of being a role model. I think a lot of guys don't want to be a role model because they never saw one. And when there wasn't one in your life it's hard to believe that they're really authentic. You see so many guys, whether they're in politics, whether they're in the law, whether they're in sports, and you hear something great about them, and then, oh man, all of a sudden, *BOOM*—this happens, or that happens. They cheated on this, or they stole that, or they lied about that.

"So after a while, we go, 'Now what?' Sooner or later people feel something is going to come out. The cynicism and sarcasm is there in our society, so for me, the most important thing is that you've got to be consistent. Be consistent and that will take care of everything else."

Singletary has had a lot of time to reflect on the most meaningful games of his career, and he cited two games that resonate strongly.

December 12, 1982

THE KINGDOME
SEATTLE SEAHAWKS 20 - CHICAGO BEARS 14
By Mike Singletary

It was my second year in the league, and that was the strike year. We weren't very good that year and finished 3-6. We were playing Seattle in Seattle, and we weren't doing very well. But there was a particular time in the game when we stiffened on defense and kept them out of the end zone. They got down to the goal line—that was when they had Jim Zorn at quarterback—and we held them out of the end zone.

For us it was the excitement of being successful in that small way. We talked about it because the Seahawks were pretty good near the goal line back then. They just wanted to run the ball, and we held. There was something about that that sparked us, the way we thought about ourselves.

On the trip back home, we talked about it some more. We said, "You know what? We kept those guys out of the end zone. Man, we were playing." We made a lot of good defensive plays in that game. They had Steve Largent, one of the great receivers, and we held him to low yardage. We were just in there fighting, and we were finding out for the first time that maybe there was something about us that could be special.

We lost the game, but what we did during the game enabled us to grow as a team. That is something you look back on—a series that sometimes a team can point to and think of as a turning point in its development.

***

When Singletary joined the Bears in 1981, they were removed from previous glory days and seeking to rebuild. The club turned to former star player Mike Ditka to change the culture and turn the Bears into a Super Bowl team. The strike year, a mess on many fronts, was Ditka's first as head coach. After that, he changed players, changed attitudes, and changed the Bears' location in the standings. By 1984, the Bears were 10-6 and were starting to think they were on the cusp of becoming part of the NFL's elite. In 1985, the Bears won the Super Bowl, and in 1986, they were smashing their way through the regular season again.

The Bears really had nothing to prove, but the swaggering defense still pursued perfection. What the players rarely did, however, was tell everybody in advance that they were going to be perfect.

October 5, 1986

THE HUBERT H. HUMPHREY METRODOME
CHICAGO BEARS 23 - MINNESOTA VIKINGS 0
By Mike Singletary

We were a pretty decent team, and we weren't doing very well in the game. Once again, we were in a goal-line situation, trying to keep the Vikings out of the end zone.

Just before that the middle finger on my left had got hurt and kind of popped out. The doctor had to take me off the field and upstairs to stitch it up, and he said, "Well, you know you guys have really fought hard. I'm going to wrap it up, and you just watch the rest of the game." And I said, "Well, I'm not watching the rest of the game. I'm gonna play." He said, "This is really foolish, but okay."

The doctor went ahead and wrapped up my finger and hand. The bandage looked like a boxing glove. I went back downstairs to the sideline, and sure enough when I got back there, it was a goal-line situation. Our punter had fumbled the ball inside the five-yard line. When I got put back into the game, I walked right through the Vikings huddle and told them, "You will not score."

Their first reaction was, "What the heck are you doing in our huddle telling us this?" One of their guys—I can't remember who now—said, "You know what? I'll tell you what. I'll make you a bet. We will score." And I said right back to him, "I'm telling you, you will not." They had four downs to get into the end zone, and they didn't score. We turned the game around and won, which was huge.

I have no idea where it came from for me to do such a thing. It was just one of those things. I can't even explain it. I don't know what it really was. It was suggested that maybe I had a lot of emotion because of the injury, but I don't know. Every now and then, you just do things like that. I guess it was just being extra fired up.

As a coach, if one of my guys did that to the opposition, I would think, "Hey, you know what? I've got a player."

***

Singletary was a definite leader on the field, and he was the type of player from whom other players took their cues and also admired. When Singletary was playing, he was the type of guy people looked at and said he would make a great coach someday. Indeed, Singletary was still a player when he decided he wanted to stay in football after retirement and become the leader of his own team. But then he changed his mind for a little while.

"Originally, when I was playing, I wanted to become a coach," Singletary said. "I thought of all of the coaches who had made a difference in my life and I thought I certainly wanted to coach and kind of pass it on. But towards the end of my career I talked to several coaches. Buddy Ryan, our defensive coordinator, said, 'You don't want to coach. You want to be a commissioner or something else in the sport. You want to own a team or something like that, but you don't want to coach. You've got too many skills.'

"There were a lot of people trying to talk me out of it, even the one who had asked me to come and coach for him when I retired," Singletary continued. "My last year playing I began to ask coaches, 'How do you balance family life and being a great coach?' They said, 'You had better get a great wife because you're not really gonna be there a lot, and she's going to have to be able to manage a lot of things. You're gonna miss the kids a lot.'"

Singletary was disappointed by the answers, and they made him think about his future. He was very proud of being a father and wanted to be very involved in his kids' lives. He decided coaching was the wrong track for him.

"I thought, 'You know, it's not worth it to me,'" Singletary said. "I got married to be a husband and be a father to my kids, and nothing is worth missing all of that."

Singletary let a decade pass between his retirement as an active player and his return to the sport as an assistant coach. His kids grew up some; at 45, he had matured even more—but felt he still harbored the ambition to lead a team. As promised, being a coach is demandingly time-consuming, requiring time away from home, but Singletary is making it all work.

"I don't even count the hours," Singletary said while working with the 49ers. "I just know that what happens is that my wife and I always talk about each week and look at what it takes to be successful with the team and at the same time be successful at home. So far, whether we have been in Baltimore or San Francisco, both head coaches [Brian Billick and Mike Nolan] have been very family friendly. So I get to see the kids a lot. I make the effort."

Yet during the football season, Singletary does work seven days a week—at least part of each day.

"Sunday is, of course, game day," Singletary said. "Saturday is a little different. If you're at home, that's a great day. Friday is a great day. Thursday is a great day. They're average workdays. Monday, Tuesday, and Wednesday are a little later. It works out very well for us. Thankfully, I'm not with a team where you have to work until two o'clock in the morning every night. That, to me, would not be worth it, and those jobs do exist."

Singletary's latest book, *Singletary One-on-One*, offers insights into some of the ex-player's thinking on such work-versus-private life issues. Singletary's earliest writings focused on the Super Bowl year and his playing career. This book, released during the 2005 season, mixes football stories with spiritual thoughts and social commentary.

"This book is more about life from a spiritual standpoint," Singletary said, "as I look at my own life with little pit stops here and there. Little stories that really sort of encourage people, who when they have tough times, when setbacks happen, are shown that there's a way to look at things. We need to find a way to work through it. There are many stories throughout the book that basically address how you can be positive and use the word of God and the stories to gain perspective.

"It intertwines football, marriage, kids, and relationships. There is a chapter that talks about being a role model. As a coach, I try to relate it to the players. They listen. As a matter of fact, they welcome it. But to truly be a role model you have to be someone who lives the right way all of the time. You have to be consistent. You have to be consistent in the way you coach, the way you treat your family, in the way you live, and even during the highs and lows of games. In the beginning, the players keep watching you. It's as if they're looking for something, for a flaw to appear."

Now that Singletary is back in the game working as an assistant coach, he has rekindled the desire to become a head coach. One day he wants to be the captain of his own ship, applying all of his football knowledge and the lessons he has learned in life to making a team a winner, turning a team into a Super Bowl champion.

"I definitely want to run my own team," Singletary said, "if it's the Lord's will. I'm excited about the opportunity. I have worked as an assistant coach in San Francisco, and I will just continue to work and learn and understand everything that I need to do. My goal is to be one of the greatest coaches of all time. That's my goal.

"It was great for me to be coached by Mike Ditka and Buddy Ryan at the same time. No doubt we should have won about three Super Bowls. I learned a great deal about continuity, about all types of disruptions and things that take away your focus. You've got to stay focused."

The best thing of all for Singletary would be a return to Chicago to become the head coach and then lead his old team to a Super Bowl championship. One of these days that just might happen.

19

RICHARD DENT

The players who give quarterbacks the heebie-jeebies throughout their careers and long into retirements are the big, fast guys with the tricky moves whose specialty is rushing the passer—the defenders who streak past blockers and level quarterbacks. They squash passers, break bones, destroy offenses, and disrupt game plans by sacking the QB.

The word "sack"—as a description of the way these rushers plunder quarterbacks, smashing them to the turf—is both violent and impersonal, but ever-so-perfect in meaning. The tacklers upend the passer like a sack of potatoes. Few have ever been better at this specialty than Bears defensive end Richard Dent. Not only did Dent have the speed and power to evade offensive linemen and make quarterbacks' lives hell, he had the drive to do it over and over again. Several times Dent was photographed flying through the air like a missile, arms extended, feet trailing, about to pulverize a passer. Gazing at the picture, one pities the poor quarterback about to be blindsided, and thinks, "Ooh … that's gonna leave a mark."

Richard Lamar Dent was born December 13, 1960, in Atlanta, Georgia, and he played college football at Tennessee State, where he majored in commercial arts and minored in bashing quarterbacks. Even in college, Dent was a sackmaster, recording a school record with 39.

Perhaps because he played at a smaller school, Dent was overlooked in the NFL player draft of 1983. Team after team passed on him before the Bears selected Dent with their eighth-round pick.

A defensive end who stood 6-foot-5 and whose playing weight was about 265 pounds, Dent terrorized offensive linemen in the NFL for 15 seasons. He spent from 1983 through 1993 with the Bears and finished his career in 1997 after stints with San Francisco, the Bears again, Indianapolis, and Philadelphia. During his 203-game NFL career, Dent amassed 137 ½ sacks and remains the Bears' record-holder in the category.

Dent was never better than during the Bears' great Super Bowl season of 1985. That season he accumulated a startling 17 sacks and forced seven fumbles. That meant he left quarterbacks black and blue and also humiliated all ball carriers. Dent also forced two fumbles and came through with one and a half sacks in the Super Bowl and was named the game's Most Valuable Player after Chicago's 46-10 triumph over New England.

"When I was a little kid I wanted to be a football player and be someone people looked up to," Dent said on a Chicago radio show during the 2005 season.

He did both. But only after he dabbled in golf as a youngster because of an uncle who caddied for big-time professionals like Gary Player. Football turned out to be the right path, though, for a player now receiving Hall of Fame consideration.

Dent had many outstanding games during the Super Bowl season, but the contests he favors occurred the season before, when the Bears were on the verge of a breakthrough and becoming recognized as a top NFL club.

Pass rusher supreme, Richard Dent gave opposing quarterbacks nightmares from his visits to their backfield. He has remained active in the Chicago area with many worthy causes. *Photo by Jonathan Daniel/Getty Images*

December 30, 1984

ROBERT F. KENNEDY STADIUM
CHICAGO BEARS 23 - WASHINGTON REDSKINS 19
By Richard Dent

The one game that always stands out for me is the playoff game against the Washington Redskins. They were coached by Joe Gibbs—his first time around—and they had been a top team in the NFC for a while. Beating the Redskins, in Washington, showed us what we could be. It was the first round of the playoffs, and the Bears hadn't won a playoff game in years.

It was a very good indication of how great a team we could be and how physical we were if we played our hearts out. It was one of those killer moments that we had. Someone told me that Joe Theisman said on some video that he still dreams about me coming after him. I don't know about that, but it made me laugh. But a tough rush was a nightmare for quarterbacks, and we wanted to get into the minds of quarterbacks and keep ourselves there and make them think.

The thing I liked best about being a pass rusher was having the ability to maybe change the game and take the ball away from the quarterback, to make a difference in the outcome by making a sack. After a while, I got bored with sacks. I wanted the ball. If I could get into the backfield faster, I could knock the ball out of the quarterback's hands. I could get the ball for us, and that's what I wanted. I wanted the big plays to make a difference in the result. Getting turnovers usually made that kind of difference.

I played a good game against the Redskins that day and I also played the mind game. I was playing off the side of the guard and I understood where the double-team was coming from. If Joe Theisman still thinks about that, it means I did a good job and played hard.

***

A year after the Redskins playoff win, with confidence gained, the Bears blitzed the entire league—and the defense set the tone.

"We seemed to come into our own after that," Dent said. "And when we won the Super Bowl, it was the defense that led the league. We were very proud of what we did on defense."

Dent still lives in the Chicago area and stays in shape with a variety of sporting pursuits from racquetball to tennis, to swimming and horseback riding. Dent operates both a business and a charitable foundation. His company, RLD Resources, handles fuel management and communications and has supervised the gas use in the Chicago Public School system in order to save operations money.

His Make-A-Dent Foundation started a scholarship fund at Columbia College and raised $50,000 for the school's sports management program in support of diversity. In 1992, Dent committed to fundraising in order to construct permament housing for homeless families. At the time, Dent said, "Chicago has given me a great opportunity as a player. This is something I can do for Chicago."

All of those reasons support the notion that Dent has realized another of his childhood goals—making people look up to him.

Although close to the city and the fans, at times Dent, who later in his career was hampered by bad knees, felt underappreciated by Bears officials. When he was waived and moved on to San Francisco at the end of his career, Dent expressed his displeasure with management. The relationship experienced signs of renewal when Dent broke away from his business interests for a season and rejoined the Bears as a defensive line coach under Dick Jauron in 2003. Jauron called Dent "a great pass rusher" with the skill and credibility to pass on his knowledge to young players just learning the pro game as defensive ends.

When Dent was asked about his ability to get techniques across to those young players, Dent said, "I've kicked every can that every player will be kicking."

Dent was one of the first tutors of draft picks Alex Brown from Florida and Michael Haynes from Penn State. However, when Jauron was fired after that season, Dent was out of a football coaching job.

Given that Dent is one of the all-time greatest pass rushers—he was fifth on the career list of sackmeisters when he retired—it would seem likely that he will soon pick up the phone and find the Hall of Fame on the other end inviting him to join the exclusive club.

Since 2003, Dent has been a regular on the list of 15 finalists, but he was still waiting to be chosen. Coach Mike Ditka said his man is definitely a Hall of Famer. Fans and long-time observers of the Bears think it is only a matter of time before Dent's turn comes.

"Other people talk about it," he said.

Since selection to the Hall of Fame is the grandest individual honor any athlete can hope for, it would be difficult for Dent to wipe out all thoughts of his possible election, but he says he tries not to think about it much.

"I don't really worry about it," Dent said, "because I have no control over it. My work is done." As he said to an interviewer once, his Tennessee State coach John Merritt always used to note, "The hay is in the barn."

No, Dent will not be adding to his sack total anytime soon unless he bumps into Troy Aikman or Joe Theisman at an old-timer's cocktail party and shows off the form that kept them awake nights.

Dent's community involvment and the foundation that is making a dent is work that is just beginning. His imposing number of sacks and his overall performance for the Bears and other teams over a long career—should represent enough football work for Richard Dent to be welcomed into the Hall of Fame.

20

TIM WRIGHTMAN

That anyone connected with the Super Bowl Bears had as much fun on and off the field as Tim Wrightman is hard to imagine. Since that team had more laughs than an elementary school class at Disneyland, there was plenty of competition. It would be easy to say that a guy who dabbled in stand-up comedy while he was a pro football player and went off to act in Hollywood after he was finished bashing people around could be characterized as the wrong man for the sport; but Wrightman was the right man at the right time for many key Chicago games.

Wrightman was a rookie during the 1985 Super Bowl season and played just one more pro season. His two years in the National Football League, both of them with the Bears, were very productive, even while sharing his position with Emery Moorehead. Prior to joining the Bears, however, Wrightman was an All-American at UCLA and also played for the Chicago Blitz in the United States Football League.

The Blitz became the Arizona Wranglers, and Wrightman was put out of commission with an injury. Wrightman had been drafted by the Bears in the third round in 1982, but chose to play in the upstart league. The first meaningful contact Wrightman had with the Bears after that came via phone call in January 1985. He was back home in California playing touch football in a park with some actor friends on Super Bowl Sunday.

"I remember saying, 'We've got to cut off the game early because the Super Bowl starts in an hour,'" Wrightman said. "One year later, I'm in the Super Bowl with the Bears."

Timothy John Wrightman was born March 27, 1960, in Los Angeles, California. He played high school ball at Mary Star of the Sea High School in San Pedro, California, before matriculating at UCLA where he set pass-catching records. As a 6-foot-3, 237-pound tight end, Wrightman put up solid numbers with the Bears. He caught 24 passes averaging 17 yards per catch—extraordinarily high for a tight end—during the Super Bowl season. The next season, Wrightman caught 22 passes.

Wrightman never really seemed destined to play for the Bears. His draft year was ancient history; he had been injured; and when he got the invitation to join the Bears for training camp during the summer of 1985, the chances of his making the team seemed slim.

"It was pretty amazing," Wrightman said. "When I came to the NFL, I was damaged goods. I had already had three knee surgeries. The Bears were the only team willing to take a chance on me. They probably figured, 'Well, we've wasted a draft pick on him; we might as well bring him in as a free agent.'"

When Wrightman showed up, he was listed seventh on the depth chart at tight end. That is like going to a Major League team's spring training and finding yourself listed seventh in line for the second-base job.

"They had Emery and Pat Dunsmore [who had played the preceding two years], two other three other guys they brought in as free agents, and me," Wrightman said. "I was like number seven. I thought, 'Well, cream rises to the top.' As training camp went along, guys got cut, guys got hurt, guys who had been there before were injured and went on the injured reserve list. By the beginning of the season, Emery and I were the only two healthy tight ends."

He dabbled in standup comedy, became an actor in Hollywood, and now spends much of his time hunting in Idaho, but during his two years with the Bears, Tim Wrightman shared the tight end spot and produced key catches.
Photo by Jonathan Daniel/Getty Images

Surprisingly, Wrightman did make the team—not just any team in the NFL, either, but a team that was headed to the Super Bowl. Still, he had to wonder how much he was going to play. At that point, Moorehead was obviously the starter, the number-one guy. But Wrightman made inroads when thrown onto the field. Some Bear formations called for the use of two tight ends, too, so Wrightman got some minutes.

In the sixth game of the season, with things going swimmingly for the Bears, Wrightman proved the value of being both healthy and in the right place at the right time, and how seizing opportunity when it is offered can provide major dividends. That he considers this the Bears game of his life is no wonder—it led to all of his future success.

October 13, 1985

CANDLESTICK PARK
CHICAGO BEARS 26 - SAN FRANCISCO 49ERS 10
By Tim Wrightman

This was a rematch of the game for the NFC championship the year before when the 49ers beat the Bears very badly (23-0). I wasn't there then, but I knew the history.

By then, I was second on the depth chart. I had been playing for a while with professional teams, so I wasn't really a novice, and I got some chances and was catching a lot of balls in the two-tight-end formations. We still had only two tight ends on the roster. But Emery got hurt that week, and I was the only tight end. They figured they had to use me.

I didn't know until just before the game Emery wasn't going to play at all. I was looking around for my helmet thinking I better suit up and get ready. But as it turned out, I went into the game with the offense on the first possession, and I had a great game. I caught three balls for about 87 yards, and I had a really terrific game blocking. That was the turning point of my career with the Bears. After that, I started playing more. I split time with Emery. It was a big day for me. I got a chance to play, and I proved that I could.

I usually got a good amount of yardage with my catches, but I didn't have breakaway speed. But you can look at the films, and sometimes I knew my most effective move was to run over the defender. On the films, you'll see me running away from guys with the tackling angle. Sometimes I figured I had a better chance of running over them and getting more yardage. Otherwise, the defender would catch me from behind.

At various times, Coach Ditka told me I reminded him of him. Mike was a great tight end, the best of his time. Before I was drafted by the Bears—while still at UCLA—one of the old-time scouts, Fido Murphy, used to come by and say, "Oh, the Bears are going to take you, Tim." Everybody else told me, "Nah, you can't believe what Fido is saying. He's just kept on with the Bears because he's one of George Halas' old guys."

"Fido said, 'Mike's looked at the films. You remind him a lot of him. You run hard. You have great hands. You're a tenacious blocker.' He was right. It came true."

***

Wrightman had a blast with those Bears. Who wouldn't? Not only did the Bears become world champs, they had fun-loving players, were adored in Chicago, and became a cultural phenomenon outside their home base. More than one writer or player has made the analogy that when the Bears showed up for a game, it was like the circus coming to town.

"I've got this drawing from the year after the Super Bowl from a sports magazine," Wrightman said. "It has the theme of the circus coming to town. It showed Ditka as a ringleader; and Payton as a strong man; and Doug Flutie playing a little flute. It's got all of these cartoon-like characters, and that's what it was. I have a clown face on because I used to do comedy. You've got Willie Gault with his head sticking out of a cannon. It's funny. It's kind of interesting, but that's what it was—the circus coming to town. People who didn't even follow professional football paid attention to us."

And not only in the United States—during the 1986 preseason, the Bears hit the road, or rather the friendly skies, to play an exhibition game called the American Bowl in England against the Dallas Cowboys.

"When we got off the plane," Wrightman said, "immediately there were shouts of 'The Fridge! The Fridge! Where's The Fridge?' People who didn't pay attention to the football on the field knew about The Fridge. William Perry became a phenomenon because he was large and played offense, and he had that gap-toothed smile. And people knew about Jim McMahon doing his crazy stuff and wearing the headbands. Women who didn't know anything about football would talk about The Fridge and the Bears. It was fun."

Wrightman was a big-city guy at the time, oriented towards the bright lights. He said he is happy he didn't sign with a small-market team where the sidewalks were rolled up while the night was young.

"I'm glad I went to Chicago," he said. "It would have been a little difficult for me after having been in Los Angeles and then going to a small place. That would have been tough, but Chicago was really great. Looking back, I wish that things had worked out for me and the Bears right from the start when I was drafted. But general manager Jim Finks and I were so far apart it just didn't make sense financially for me."

Wrightman's post-USFL chance came along at the perfect moment, however. How many players would have killed to become members of a team rolling along the superhighway to the Super Bowl?

"The thing that makes me feel really good about that," Wrightman said, "is I was able to contribute, too, not just be along for the ride, but to actually contribute to the team. I went from adversity to overcome injury at the beginning of the season, to making the team, and being part of how it ended up that year was just an awesome feeling.

"We had a dominating defense, and it was interesting that we were overshadowed on offense, but if we had a team that didn't have such a tremendous defense, maybe we would have been the stars."

The 1985 Bears defense was so good that sometimes those guys felt they were winning the championship all by themselves. But the offense scored a lot, spotlighted Walter Payton running the ball, and took advantage with timely plays to demoralize the opposition.

"The defense is kind of what we're remembered for," Wrightman said. "It's true that in a lot of ways we were two separate teams until Sunday. During practice, the defensive guys were sort of like, 'Hey, offense, can you not mess up so we can win?' That kind of thing. I'd never been on a team before where there was that much competition during the week, for either the limelight or whatever. Then we came together and really played well as a team on Sunday."

The Bears needed that solidarity in order to take the upper hand in their long rivalry with the Green Bay Packers. The teams have experienced alternating dominance over the decades, but the mid-1980s was a Bears high point. In Wrightman's two seasons the Bears beat the Packers all four games. This was the most heated time in ages, when Bears coach Mike Ditka and Packers coach Forrest Gregg, one-time rivals as players, were howling rivals on the sidelines.

"They were probaby the dirtiest team we played," Wrightman said. "Packers games were the only ones I've ever been in, the only team I've ever played against, where guys actually hit [you] in the nuts. They were just trying to overcome their lack of talent."

During his Bears playing days, Wrightman became the emcee at a comedy club and did standup routines. When he retired after one too many knee problems—he had six surgeries by then—he returned to California and began acting in TV commercials and in guest spots on TV shows like *Walker, Texas Ranger,* and *Mad About You.*

A couple of years ago, weary of constant auditions, a more laidback Wrightman decided to turn the clock back to his youthful outdoor participation days. He moved to a 5,000-person community in Idaho, where he owns the 150-acre Lazy Bear Ranch, and converted an old barn to a lodge. Wrightman, who bagged a grizzly bear in Alaska, hunts for waterfowl, deer, and other wildlife. In 2005, he introduced a visitor package for clients that tied together two of his passions: hunting and football.

On autumn weekends, clients can mix hunting opportunities and watching televised football games in a rustic surrounding with Wrightman and other story-telling guest hosts that were former NFL players. It might be said that Wrightman's "Bears and Birds Weekend" features punt, pass, and shoot.

21

JAY HILGENBERG

His career was spent looking at the world upside down. Well, some of the time, at least—when Jay Hilgenberg had to look between his legs before hiking the football. Hilgenberg came from a football family of centers. Apparently, something in the genes enabled the Hilgenberg clan to grow larger than Midwest farm crops while possessing sure hands.

Fewer football-playing kids dream of playing center than any other position, and fewer big linemen are suited to playing the position than any other spot. Defensive tackles get to smash people and use their hands while doing it. Other offensive linemen just have to concentrate on blocking. The center must hold the ball rock steady, not move it an inch or be whistled for trying to draw the defense offside or for another infraction. He must have the patience to get the ball into the quarterback's hands properly, but have the reaction time to immediately focus on the next task—blocking.

Hilgenberg was born in Iowa City, Iowa, played his high school ball right there in the same city, and then played collegiately at the University of Iowa. He is the son of former Minnesota Vikings all-star linebacker Wally Hilgenberg, who also played collegiately for the Hawkeyes. Jay's older brother Jim preceded him at center at Iowa. Jay's younger brother Joel followed in both of their footsteps—and hand prints—at Iowa, and was a mainstay center for the New Orleans Saints. This brother act became as well known in the family business of hiking the pigskin as the Smothers Brothers were in comedy.

Jay Walter Hilgenberg was born March 21, 1959, and was considered a genial fellow unless colliding with other football players of approximately the same 6 feet, 3 inches, and 259 pounds he brought to the field. Hilgenberg was not only a regular for most of his 13-year career in the line, he also had the skills to hold down the job of long snapper. That singular discipline is more often manned these days by a specialist who does nothing else besides hike the ball to the holder for extra points and field goals—or to send it deep to the punter.

Hilgenberg, who still lives in the Chicago suburbs, joined the Bears as a free agent for the 1981 season and stuck with Chicago through the 1991 campaign, then wrapped up his National Football League with single seasons with the Cleveland Browns and the New Orleans Saints.

"My first year, I was the long snapper," Hilgenberg said of his rookie season, "the extra-point guy. My second year, we only played nine games because it was the strike year. I was still the snapper. That role has evolved. It's best to be invisible in that role. You don't want anybody noticing you unless you're making tackles or recovering fumbles. I tell you, the punt team is the fun thing to be on.

"On the punt team, you run down and try to make a tackle. I loved it. It was always kind of fun to go downfield and try to make a big hit, a big tackle, and then have your defense come on the field, and if you had a big hit, they'd always congratulate you. It was always cool. I'm sure the coaches take note of it when you do something like that. Dan Hampton, our defensive end, always would pump a guy up after a big hit."

It took a couple of seasons for Hilgenberg to play regularly; and even if special teams were fun, when he got his chance to start in 1983,

Jay Hilgenberg grew up in a family of football players—most of them centers—and anchored the center of the Bears line during his prime in the 1980s.
Photo by Jonathan Daniel/Getty Images

he was ready and anxious. The game of his life was the first time Hilgenberg played a considerable amount of time in a regular-season NFL game.

September 11, 1983

SOLDIER FIELD
CHICAGO BEARS 17 - TAMPA BAY BUCCANEERS 10
By Jay Hilgenberg

At the beginning of the year, I was not the starting center. I played in the second and fourth quarters, alternating with Dan Neal. Except in the second game of the year, against Tampa Bay, I got a chance to play a lot. It was extremely hot out—I remember that. The challenge in that game was blocking the Buccaneers' all-pro linebacker Dave Logan. Maybe Ditka gave me the chance because he felt like I matched up better against Logan.

Logan was a real quick guy, and the first play was an off-tackle play. He came off the ball, then took my momentum and used it against me to just toss me to the play side. I hit the ground and bounced back up and turned around to go after him. But all I could see was Walter Payton, and he had that long stride where he put his foot up in the air now and then. He's comin, doing that right in front of me. I'm trying to get out of the way, but I just caught his knee on my shoulder pad; and he went down.

I thought, "On my first play, I'm tackling Walter Payton." It was not supposed to work that way. He was on my side. Payton told me, "Hey, next time just stay on the ground." I knew my role. Things got better after that. I got more comfortable.

The game against Tampa was my first meaningful time on the offensive line, but I started the second half of the season. Dan Neal hurt his back, so I started the final eight games. The team was improving. I know we went 3-5 the first half that year, and then the last half we went 5-3. We actually won five of our last six games.

In the ninth game of the season, our second game against Detroit, which we lost 38-17, I almost recovered a football for a touchdown. Our quarterback, Vince Evans, was scrambling, and the ball bounced loose. He was running up the middle. When I saw he was going to run, I turned to look for a block. Next thing I know, the ball was bouncing right to the end zone. I went right up to the end zone after the ball, but I missed it. I don't think I got a hand on it. I remember thinking that I hadn't reacted as quickly as I had hoped. I was so close to getting it. I felt like I should have had the fumble for a touchdown. I remember thinking at the time that, as an offensive lineman, it might be as close to a touchdown in the NFL as I ever got in my life—and it was.

We had a couple of wars with the Packers. The last game of the season we won 23-21 in Chicago, but it was so cold that day. They scored late in the game to go ahead of us. We used like a two-minute offense to go downfield. I was so cold on the field that I remember thinking, "If we win this game, I'm going down to the most southern part of the United States on vacation immediately." Oh, I was ready to go someplace warm. And I did go on vacation to warm up—down to Key West.

***

One of the most peculiar plays Hilgenberg was ever involved in took place during the 1982 season. The Bears were playing the Cardinals, then still located in St. Louis.

"I was the long snapper, and I recovered a fumble," Hilgenberg said. "The punter got hit, and the ball bounced in the air. I caught it in the air on about the 15-yard line. All I had was about 15 yards to run for a touchdown. There was only one guy in front of me and another guy lying on the ground. I tripped over him. I was thinking, 'Man. ...'

"Once we regained possession down there, we couldn't move it any closer to the goal line. I went into the game to snap the ball for a field goal attempt, and the field goal kicker hit me with the ball when he tried to kick it. That was kind of the insult to injury. We lost that game 10-7."

By 1983, even though they only finished 8-8, the Bears recognized that they had talent to build upon on the roster. The strong finish helped the long-term attitude.

"We definitely felt we were improving," Hilgenberg said.

Even the year before Mike Ditka's Bears were starting to sense the bad old days were on the verge of becoming old news. Then along came the strike, and it disrupted everything he was trying to build. The 1982 strike season was so wacky that, when the Bears were 3-5, all they had to do was beat Tampa Bay in the season's final game to finish 4-5; which would have advanced them to the playoffs.

"We got beat by a field goal," Hilgenberg said of the 26-23 loss to the Buccaneers. "It was such a weird year. But we could feel the building blocks were starting to be in place. We had a lot of great players for a young group, and it was together for a few years, so that helped. We got some confidence and started going."

It is often said in professional sports that if a team is not acquiring more talent, or showing growth, that it is standing still, and other teams will move ahead of them no matter how good they looked before or on paper.

"You always have to get better," Hilgenberg said. "Each week you have to improve. As an athlete, there's no leveling off. If you don't try to get better, people keep passing you. It's like in golf. You've got to make birdies. You don't win tournaments by making pars."

Payton was just about the biggest star in the NFL as the Bears matured into Super Bowl champions; clearly, if you were a young lineman trying to find your place as a starter with the Bears, you had better do a good job for him. Despite Hilgenberg's inauspicious start, he said Payton's work habits made him easy to work with. The defense may not have known where he was going, but the linemen did.

"He was an easy guy to block for because, if the play was called to the four hole or the five hole, you knew he was going to be at the hole that was called," Hilgenberg said. "And that he was going to get there with a lot of power. For an offensive lineman, you can't ask for much more than that. Being where you're supposed to be when the play is called. He was always there so you could get quick leverage on the defensive line. It was a very aggressive running style. My game was quickness. I had two strong guards on either side of me, and people knew we were going to run the ball. We weren't trying to do too much offensively besides that."

The defense got way more publicity than the offense during the Bears' Super Bowl season, but the lot of an offensive lineman is to be anonymous, even when things are going well. Hilgenberg figures the public almost never heard about him, but that was okay.

"Any time you hear about offensive linemen too much, it's usually because something bad is going on," he said.

During the Super Bowl season, the Bears gradually took on an air of invincibility. By the time the playoffs began, it seemed unlikely that they would lose. By the time they reached the Super Bowl, it seemed it would be impossible for the Bears to lose. Never mind that they had defeated the Patriots by just 13 points early in the season. Chicago believed it was a far superior team in January than at the time of their September meeting. The Bears also felt the two-week bye between conference championships and the Super Bowl game was an advantage.

"We had two weeks to get ready to play the game," Hilgenberg said. "We were so prepared for them. I felt, in the actual Super Bowl, that there was no way we would lose that game. They played a three-four defense, and no one could play a three-four defense against us."

Certainly no one could play with those Bears—regardless of offense or defense.

22

KEITH VAN HORNE

Gazing upon Keith Van Horne's mammoth physique could be intimidating. He was a big guy playing a football position where they are all big guys. He just didn't seem to be a guy you wanted flexing his muscles in your face.

Van Horne is 6-foot-6, and his playing weight with the Bears of the 1980s and 1990s was around 280 pounds. A generation later, offensive tackles like Van Horne commonly weigh 50 pounds more. They look more like sumo blockers than sculpted athletes, and although they are strong and fast, the tackles of Van Horne's era seemed more fearsome because they looked like football players.

There are few times in an offensive lineman's career when recognition comes easily. Guards and tackles do not carry the ball, most of their key blocks occur in the scrimmages along the line where a few tons of beef is growling, scratching, shoving, and gouging— impossible to observe closely, even with binoculars. Fans know those players' jersey numbers, but usually not their faces.

Yet Van Horne had the good fortunate to play for a team that won a Super Bowl—a team that was renowned for its strong personality as well as its outstanding won-loss record. More than two decades later, the team's fans still revere the players who won the 1986 Super Bowl.

It doesn't hurt any that Van Horne still lives in the Chicago area and has done some Bears pregame broadcasting, keeping his voice out there. During his playing days, Van Horne's weight carried the man. Now his name carries the weight.

"Once a Bear, always a Bear," Van Horne said of the pleasant way fans recall his two-decade-old contributions. "It's amazing how the community reacts. During our 20th-anniversary celebrations of winning the Super Bowl during the 1985 season, there were still endorsement opportunities out there for us and opportunities where people wanted us to speak and come to dinners and events. It's an amazing thing 20 years later. You know they love their 1985 Bears."

Keith Van Horne was born November 6, 1957, in Mount Lebanon, Pennsylvania; but played his high school football in Fullerton, California. He became a star lineman for the University of Southern California, earned All-America mention, and was runner-up in the voting for the Outland Trophy as college football's most outstanding lineman. Van Horne was the Bears' number-one draft choice in 1981. He played his entire 13-season career through 1993 for the Bears, participating in 186 games. His brother Pete, a first-baseman-outfielder, was a Chicago Cubs draft pick.

Perhaps Bears fans' love affair with the 1985 team would be tempered if either that squad continued to win more Super Bowls (Van Horne feels they should have won at least three) with some fresh players, or any Bears team had captured a championship before the 20th reunion rolled around. But in a city where pro football is king, fans remain fondly grateful to the Bears who brought so much excitement to town.

"They love the Bears," Van Horne said of the fans. "I mean a Bears fan is a Bears fan. But they have a special place in their hearts for us, and we certainly appreciate that. It's quite a blessing to be able to have those opportunities still 20 years down the road. It's really neat."

Van Horne sorted out the favorite games of his career long ago by meaning, accomplishment, and what they did to help make his team into a champion.

Offensive lineman Keith Van Horne, another veteran of the 1985 title team, marvels at the continuing devotion of Bears fans to that team and basks in the glow of love for the champs. *Photo by Jonathan Daniel/Getty Images*

November 4, 1984

SOLDIER FIELD
CHICAGO BEARS 17 - LOS ANGELES RAIDERS 6
By Keith Van Horne

The 1984 game against the Raiders at home was a big win for us. They were the defending champions. Kurt Becker, the starting right guard, and me, the starting right tackle, played great games on that side of the line. Howie Long, a damned good player for the Raiders, was quoted after the game as saying he hadn't been beaten up like that since grade school.

So Kurt Becker and I took it to him that day. That one is a game that helped establish us as up-and-coming, a legitimate team. It does matter who you beat to make a statement. That season we finished 10-6 and made the playoffs. And we won the wild-card game in Washington against the Redskins. That was a great game, too. Then, of course, we got our asses handed to us by San Francisco. But overall that was another step we took towards actually believing in ourselves.

Those games with the Raiders, the Redskins, and even losing to the 49ers 23-0, worked the same way. They were definite contributors to our growth. We just realized what it took to get to the next level. I think maybe that's what was in our minds going into the off-season and leading up to 1985. All three games did the same thing. They were different. We won, we lost, we got our heads handed to us. But I think there was value in all of them.

The Raiders game was the first one. Although they had some new players, they were the defending champions; and we were a young team.

✳✳✳

When the Bears gathered for the 1985 season under Mike Ditka, they were more of a grown-up team from the previous year. Nobody around the NFL, however, expected Chicago to burst out of the gate and win every game. For a while, though, it appeared Chicago might go undefeated. The Bears won their first 12 games that season, but not all came easily. That's where the toughening-up process of 1984 contributed, Van Horne thinks.

"I think we had to come from behind to win all of our first five games," Van Horne. "Maybe I'm mistaken; maybe not five. But it seemed as if it was happening every week. That was the beginning of the year, and it usually takes the offense longer to click. The defense was keeping us in games. Then we were able to capitalize on that. We got the confidence and momentum going, and it took off from there."

One of those true momentum-setters was a stunning performance mid-way through the season.

November 17, 1985

TEXAS STADIUM
CHICAGO BEARS 44 - DALLAS COWBOYS 0
By Keith Van Horne

That was spectacular just because it was the Cowboys. They were "America's team"—I always hated that phrase. And then, of course Mike had played and coached there, so he was all fired up to do it at Dallas and to America's team.

We dethroned them, and we became America's team. That was a very enjoyable thing. We ran all over them on offense, and we beat them up on defense. That game really sticks out in my mind.

The defense got a lot of the praise that season, but we had Walter Payton on offense. He could do just about anything. It was an honor to block for him, a pleasure. He kept you on your game. I'll tell you what: if you didn't do your job, you got a stare from Walter Payton. He reminded you if you didn't do something right, and he kept you focused. He was an inspiration because he worked so hard and was such an incredible specimen.

Walter worked very hard at working out, but he was a naturally strong man as well. Put that together, and his legs were incredibly strong. To watch him just knock people over was very impressive. He attacked people. They didn't attack him, the ball carrier. They tried to, but he took it to them. It certainly makes your job easier.

You knew that if you gave Walter a crease or an opportunity, he was going to take advantage of it. He's going to see it. And you also know that he's going to be giving you his best. It makes you want to make sure you give him your best, as well.

***

Van Horne realizes that he was lucky to play with the Bears at a time when the chief rival, the Green Bay Packers, was as down and out as a Dust Bowl victim. Van Horne said the players understood the meaning and history behind the rivalry, but the Bears were ascendant, and during that mid-1980s time period, the Packers were not among the best teams in the league. They were struggling.

"Oh, we always beat Green Bay," Van Horne said. "I'm not sure it's the same now. Maybe [new coach] Lovie Smith is bringing it back. I know when Dave Wannstedt was the coach—I played with him my last year—he just thought it was another game, and that was something that upset me. I thought, 'Look, you don't get it.'"

Other new assistant coaches joined the team, and Van Horne said they didn't seem to get it either that beating Green Bay was a big deal for spectators and for controlling division play. When he took over as head coach, Smith proclaimed that beating the Packers was a goal in his meet-the-community first press conference, which resonated with the fans.

"I'm thinking, 'What's wrong with you guys?'" Van Horne said of the newcomers to the organization. "That's not a good sign. Of course, we didn't have to deal with Brett Favre when I was playing— just maybe his first year as quarterback with the Packers. He made all of the difference in turning it around for the Packers.

"Mike Ditka cranked it up a notch with Green Bay. He and Forrest Gregg, who became the Packers' coach, played against each other, and they hated each other. That carried over to the players."

Every year, as soon as the schedule is released, the two matchups with the Packers get asterisks marked against the dates in magic marker. One day, the bad guys are coming to town. The other day that's the one the team travels to the frozen north. But in 1985, it didn't seem to matter too much who the Bears played. Nearly every game was a memory-maker for a team that finished 15-1 during the regular season.

"That whole year was a highlight," Van Horne said. "It's a once-in-a-lifetime thing. There's no team that's been like that one. There will never be another team that was like that in terms of talent, or character on the field and off. Our coach was a character. It was just the way the country took us in and was rooting for us."

23

WILLIE GAULT

O ver the years, many observers outside of football have made fun of speed-demon sprint times. They scoff when they hear of assistant coaches with stop watches reporting breathless times for football players in the 100-yard dash or the 40-yard dash. Track coaches in particular have been skeptical of football timing. They just think the football coaches want their players to sound faster, just the way basketball coaches want their players to sound taller, adding a couple of inches to their height on their bio page in the annual media guide.

Once in a while, however, the genuine article comes along. A Bob Hayes, whose credentials as an Olympic gold medalist 100 man were more than reliable when he showed up as a pass receiver for the Dallas Cowboys. Running back O.J. Simpson was one of the fastest football players of all time, and he competed on the track team at Southern Cal.

In the 1960s and 1970s, some track stars with limited or non-existent football backgrounds tried to make the leap from running dashes in short pants and singlets to running with the football in shoulder pads and helmets. Many failed. Willie Gault, who attended the University of Tennessee, was the real thing. He was both football player and track star. His well-documented speed was unquestioned, and he showed enough as a college football player to tease the pros with his potential.

Gault enjoyed one of the most colorful and flashy athletic careers of the 20th century. He was an Olympian in track and field, a member of a Super Bowl-champion football team, and he was an Olympic alternate in the bobsled. It was some mix. He began early living an interesting and unique life and continues to do so today.

While still playing pro football, the supersonic runner talked about becoming a fashion designer and began an acting career when he was playing with the Bears. Once he participated in a charity fundraiser for the Better Boys Foundation by dancing with the Chicago City Ballet. He said he hesitated to accept the offer because he knew he was going to be prancing around in tights and didn't want to make a fool out of himself, but he said he enjoyed doing it.

At one point, Coach Mike Ditka wondered if his receiver was committed to the Bears and football because Gault set up residency in California in order to begin acting lessons. He said he was merely preparing for life after football and was surprised there was any criticism of his actions.

Gault, who excelled on track relay teams, was a superb high hurdler, recording times in the 13-plus-second range in the 110-meter event. He qualified for the 1980 U.S. Summer Olympic team in the 100- and 200-meter dashes, but President Jimmy Carter ordered a boycott of those Games. In 1983, Gault shared a gold medal as one of the four members of the United States world record-setting 4x100-meter relay team at the world track and field championships in Helsinki, Finland. He also won a bronze medal in the hurdles.

In the late 1980s, Gault took up bobsledding in order to be one of the few athletes to ever make the transition from the Summer Olympics to the Winter Olympics. Gault qualified as a U.S. alternate for the 1988 Winter Games in Calgary as a "pusher" in the bobsled.

Willie Gault hauled in this pass against the New England Patriots and kept on running—the thing he did best on the football field. The track and field Olympian, now an actor in Hollywood, made big catches routinely for the Bears.
Photo by Focus on Sport/Getty Images

Track star Willie Davenport had set the precedent of moving from the hurdles to bobsledding in 1980, and later running back Herschel Walker sought to make the switch.

"I wanted to be in both the Summer and Winter Olympics," Gault said. "I narrowed things down, and bobsledding was the only thing I could do in the Winter Olympics."

Gault pictured himself as neither a downhill skier nor a ski jumper, but speed plays a critical role in getting the two-man and four-man bobsled off the starting line.

"I had a great time," Gault said. "Definitely it was different, but it was great. I really enjoyed it."

Gault was an exceptional kickoff returner in college for the Volunteers and caught 50 passes one season, so he really was a do-it-all athlete at a high level. In 1990, the United States Track and Field Federation awarded Gault its Jim Thorpe All-Around Athlete Award.

Gault's speed helped him excel in the highest level of football. Jim Harbaugh, one of his Bears quarterback partners, said Gault was so quick, a thrower had to be aware of his delivery.

"Something different has to click when he's out there because he's so fast," Harbaugh said when they were playing together. "You really have to let go of it early, throw as far as you can, and let him go get it."

Willie James Gault was born September 5, 1960, in Griffin, Georgia, and revealed his athletic prowess there as a high school star before matriculating at Tennessee. By the time Gault finished recording his college achievements, the Bears came calling, making him their No. 1 draft choice in 1983. Gault joined the Bears that season, becoming a key figure as an explosive weapon during the 1985 Super Bowl season, and stayed in the NFL through 1993. His career was split between five seasons with the Bears and six seasons with the Raiders.

During his NFL career, Gault caught 333 passes, but what stood out was how his incredible speed translated to yardage after the catch. In 1985, Gault recorded a 21.3 yards-per-catch total. He truly stretched the field, opening things up for the Bears' running game. While that was a notable accomplishment during the Super Bowl season, it was routine for Gault, who retired with a per-catch average of 19.9 yards. Gault was just as effective as a kickoff returner. His Super Bowl-season average of 26.2 was second only to his final season with the Raiders, when his average hit 26.7. During the 1985 season Gault returned one kick 99 yards for a touchdown, still a record as the Bears' longest-ever kickoff return.

The game Gault chose, though, is the Super Bowl itself.

January 26, 1986

THE SUPERDOME
CHICAGO BEARS 46 - NEW ENGLAND PATRIOTS 10
By Willie Gault

The Super Bowl is something that sticks out in everyone's mind. I caught four passes for 129 yards, and I also ran back kicks for more than another 100 yards.

Winning the Super Bowl was the special highlight of my football career because it's such a huge thing. It's the Super Bowl, you know? I didn't score any touchdowns, but I helped set up one with a 60-yard catch.

People always remember "The Super Bowl Shuffle" and being in the Super Bowl. That's all people talk about, basically. It's gone by really fast. In retrospect, after the first few years it didn't seem as if time was passing so quickly, but that was 20 years ago.

It was great playing for Mike Ditka. Mike was a great coach. He played fiery, and he coached fiery. He coached exactly the way he played, with a sense of urgency. He was tough, and he wanted you to be tough, to play great. He didn't want you to make a lot of mistakes, and he coached the way he played. We didn't make a lot of mistakes.

The Bears wanted to exploit my speed. That made all of the sense in the world. When I went to the Raiders, all of the defensive backs and all of the defenders were telling me how the team would always be catering to me and making sure they knew where I was on the field. It was quite interesting to hear what other teams thought about you as a player and that they knew they had to do something to try to corral you.

***

From an early age, Gault's speed distinguished his play on the football field. Any coach with an ounce of creativity would maximize ways to put the ball into Gault's hands to put him in a position to pull off a game-breaking play. That's how Gault became so proficient at kickoff returns. He led the Southeastern Conference in kickoff returns at Tennessee, and the Bears were anxious to further his résumé.

Although Gault often returned kicks for big yardage, he ironically scored just one touchdown on a kickoff return during his entire NFL career—the 99-yarder in 1985. Gault got a kick out of returning kickoffs, though. He loved performing on the big stage, and all eyes were on him as he received the ball and hinted at the constant threat of slipping away for a long run.

September 29, 1985

SOLDIER FIELD
CHICAGO BEARS 45 - WASHINGTON REDSKINS 10
By Willie Gault

I really enjoyed kickoff returns. I did it in college, and I had a lot of success. At one point, I think I was tied for the NCAA record for most kickoff returns in a career. I had a great time. I was able to do it for part of my time in the NFL, and it was pretty fun.

One of the most memorable plays of my life was the kickoff return against the Redskins. We were down 10-0, and I ran a kickoff back for almost 100 yards. Would you believe everything snowballed after that? We went on to win the game easily. I think that win set us up for the rest of the year to go on and win the Super Bowl. Next to the Super Bowl, that was my most memorable play.

I thought I could score every time I got a kickoff. I was looking to score every time; and I was hoping I could. I was thinking I could, and I was running as if I could. It didn't work out that way, but it was always a threat, and it was always a thought in my mind.

***

Gault has always had a little bit of show business in his blood and now lives in Los Angeles where he works as an actor. He was one of the movers and shakers behind the surprise smash music video "The Super Bowl Shuffle" from the 1985 season.

He had worked on a music video for Sister Sledge, and one conversation led to another. Ten Bears sang vocals on the production, and others served as backups. Gault said approximately $250,000 was donated to charity from the video's proceeds.

After retiring from the NFL in 1993, Gault spread his wings as a performer. Among his roles was an appearance on *The West Wing*. Gault was on *The Pretenders* for three seasons, too. He also had guest starring roles on *Baywatch, In the Heat of the Night,* and *Tales From The Crypt*.

Just because Gault has changed professions doesn't mean he spends all his free time munching on junk food as a couch potato. He always watched his weight. Not long ago, at the age of 44, Gault competed in masters' hurdles races, and he said he has retained much of his speed, recording a 4.2 in the 40-yard dash.

"I still work out every day," Gault said. "It's not like I stopped cold turkey. I still get that rush."

24

JIM HARBAUGH

J im Harbaugh understands Bears town. He has seen the city go wild when the Bears were hot. He has felt the vibes when the Bears were winning. No doubt about it, when the Bears are on, Chicago is high. When the Bears are victorious, the city is happy.

"Nothing quite like it, you know?" said the former Bears quarterback of the late 1980s and early 1990s. "That community just loves, loves football. And when the Chicago Bears are playing well, there's no other city you'd rather be in or playing for—the fans are just so passionate about the game of football and knowledgeable. It goes back a long ways. The team is steeped in tradition."

Jim Harbaugh comes from a sports family, where everyone played all of the games, and then everyone coached the games. But no sport was as important as football. James Joseph Harbaugh was born December 23, 1963, in Toledo, Ohio. The family followed dad Jack's coaching career around the United States, and the younger Harbaugh played some high school ball in Ann Arbor, Michigan, and some in Palo Alto, California. Then he attended the University of Michigan, where he played for legendary coach Bo Schembechler. He placed third in the voting for the 1986 Heisman Trophy as the nation's best college player and led the Wolverines to the 1987 Rose Bowl.

Even while moving around a bit as a youth, Jim Harbaugh picked up the finer points of playing quarterback and how to be a field general, and he was the Bears' No.1 draft selection later in 1987.

Harbaugh was at his family's home in Kalamazoo, Michigan, where his father was coaching at Western Michigan University, when the Bears chose him in the player draft. He was sitting around in his pajamas watching on television because he was sick with the chicken pox. When the team called and asked him to come to Chicago for a press conference, he tried to beg off because of the illness, but the club was persuasive. Harbaugh was dotted with chicken pox spots when he arrived.

Coach Mike Ditka's first impression of Harbaugh made it sound as if he was Da Coach's kind of guy.

"I think Harbough has a great presence," Ditka said at the time. "He really feels there's nothing he can't do."

The Bears liked Harbaugh's arm strength, but his dad didn't always like his field presence when he was a youngster, telling him he was not going to make it as an athlete if he acted immaturely. Harbaugh was thrown out of a baseball game at age 10 and did not endear himself to Schembechler by showing up late for his first team meeting.

"You'll never play a down at Michigan," Schembechler told him.

Still, Harbaugh was 6 feet, 3 inches, and weighed 215 pounds; and he seemed to have all of the tools. Harbaugh began his 12-season NFL career in the fall of 1987, mostly by watching from the Bears' bench.

"I can't stand not playing," he said while waiting for the chance to beat out Jim McMahon and Mike Tomczak.

He became a regular the next season and spent seven years in Chicago before quarterbacking four years for Indianapolis, and finally a season for Baltimore in 1998. In 1995, while playing for the Colts, Harbaugh was selected for the Pro Bowl and led so many furious charges to bring his team back into games it trailed that he was nicknamed "Captain Comeback."

Harbaugh competed 58.9 percent of his passes lifetime, for 22,111 yards and 111 touchdowns. Harbaugh was also an excellent running

Jim Harbaugh grew up in a family of football players and coaches and, in 1991, turned in one of the best seasons by a Bears quarterback, throwing for 3,121 yards and 15 touchdowns. *Photo by Rick Stewart/Getty Images*

quarterback, rushing for 2,637 yards in his career with a superb 5.2 yards-per-run average. And he scored 18 touchdowns on the ground. Harbaugh's best all-around season in charge of the Bears' offense was 1991, when he completed 275 of 478 passing attempts for 3,121 yards and 15 touchdowns.

That season, too, Harbaugh played in the game of his life with the Bears.

September 23, 1991

SOLDIER FIELD
CHICAGO BEARS 19 - NEW YORK JETS 13 (OT)
By Jim Harbaugh

It was a Monday night game against the Jets. It was quite a game. We were behind in regulation. We scored a touchdown to tie it and send the game into overtime on a fourth-down play.

Before that in the fourth quarter, we got down to the New York two-yard line on one of our drives. We had a fourth-and-2, and we got stopped. The Jets took over the ball with the chance to ice the game, so they ran. They got a first down or two on the ground, but they fumbled the ball on about the 40-yard line, which gave us new life.

On that drive to tie it, I hit receiver Tom Waddle on a fourth-down pass on the sideline when we needed 18 yards for a first down. He came back towards me to get it. It was just a very dramatic game the way it went back and forth. There were seven seconds left in the game, and we were on about the four-yard line when I hit fullback Neal Anderson for a touchdown pass. There was a lot of stuff happening. I think it was a full moon or something.

In the last minute of overtime, I called a bootleg. I hit Cap Boso with the pass, and he ran to about the 1-yard line. Actually, originally on the field the officials called the play a touchdown. I remember that Cap came up from the play with a facemask full of sod. Time ran out, the game was over, the play was called a touchdown, and the teams were going into the locker room. But the officials ended up reviewing the play, and they ruled that Cap didn't score, that he was short of the goal line. So they had to bring the teams back onto the field.

Any time you have left the field, you want to keep on going and get dressed. You hate going back out, especially if you think you have won. But we had to come back, and time was an issue. There were just seconds put back on the clock. We had to score, or the game would end in a tie. At that time, the rules called for a single overtime period and then the game was declared a tie unless it was a playoff game.

On the next play, I scored a touchdown on a quarterback sneak, and we won. We won the game twice. It was an interesting finish, winning in a crazy way. So many things were going on with sending the teams to the locker room and coming back.

That was my favorite season with the Bears. We finished 11-5 and went to the playoffs. I started all 16 games. The year before I was the starter, and we had the same record, but I separated a shoulder late in the season. In 1991, we had four or five fourth-quarter comebacks besides the Jets game.

We had some good winning streaks going. We won four in a row to start the season, and we won five in a row in the middle of the season. Historically, under Mike Ditka, the Bears started fast. When you're winning a lot of games in a row, you have a very high confidence level. You feel like life is good, you know? You're playing with your friends: and there's a lot of camaraderie on the team; and you're having success. That year, 1991, was a wonderful, wonderful time in my career.

Harbaugh was an excellent athlete as a teenager, and he aspired to play professional football. Long-term, however, he also knew he wanted to make a career out of being a coach. His dad, Jack, was a long-time college assistant, and the elder Harbaugh won an NCAA I-

AA title leading Western Kentucky. Jim's older brother, John, is an assistant coach with the Philadelphia Eagles. His sister is married to Marquette men's basketball coach Tom Crean.

Upon retirement, Harbaugh immediately moved into coaching, and in 2005, he completed his second season as head football coach at the University of San Diego. Following the season, he signed a long-term deal.

"I always wanted to coach, from day one," Harbaugh said. "My dad's a coach, my brother's a coach, my brother-in-law is a coach. Tommy Crean really helps me out as a coach. To me, coaching is teaching. I started my coaching career with the Oakland Raiders. I coached there for two years and learned the craft of actually being a coach. Then the opportunity came to be a head coach. It felt right. Now my path has taken me into the college game, and I love it."

Being around football for his whole life has exposed Harbaugh to a variety of coaches and their philosophies. Between his dad's high-level college experiences, and his own playing career at Michigan and in the pros, Harbaugh met, played for, listened to, studied under, or absorbed information from a cross-section of sharp, experienced coaches.

"Bo Schembechler, Mike Ditka, Ron Turner, Lindy Infante, Ted Marchibroda, Greg Landry—so many wonderful characters and people," Harbaugh said. "I've definitely been planning for it. I used a lot of background from coaches, and I've had so many great coaches as mentors."

When Harbaugh was active in the NFL, he assimilated all of the information he learned, sifted through orders and suggestions, plays and situations, and filed them away in the back of his brain for a day he might need them or call them. He examined a circumstance and told himself, "I night be able to use that some day."

"I draw on that playing experience," Harbaugh said. "I draw on whom I played for. Even when I was playing I watched Coach Ditka, how he handled situations and the passion he brought to the game. I tried to pick up on just the football knowledge it takes to become a coach. It was always in my mind when he would be in front of the team giving a talk."

In college, Harbaugh played for the explosive, excitable, committed Schembechler. In the NFL, Harbaugh played for the explosive, excitable, committed Ditka. Both men seemed to wear their emotions on their sleeves. They seemed to hide nothing of what they were feeling as a game unfolded, of what was going through their minds at a moment when a play had gone badly or well.

"They are very similar," Harbaugh said. "You know the similarities. I hate comparing coaches, but they were so similar in their passion and love for the game of football; so similar in their competitive natures; so similar in character; and so similar in so many ways that, yeah, I always felt blessed to be playing for two living legends."

Harbaugh also shared the Bears backfield with a legend. Like anyone who got close to Walter Payton, the great runner, he discovered that Payton also had a great, wacky sense of humor.

Reminiscing in 1999, Harbaugh said when he showed up for a post-draft mini-camp Payton introduced himself dramatically.

"My first mini-camp," Harbaugh said, "the first time I got in the huddle, he pulled my shorts down. I'm standing out there in nothing but a jock strap. I was kind of like, 'Hey, Walter Payton pulled a prank on me. I feel kind of special.'"

Harbaugh said he was inspired by the work ethics of both Payton and linebacker Mike Singletary. In the NFL, it is always best for a team if the biggest stars set a good example by training hard, but it doesn't always happen.

"I've seen where the best players don't always work the hardest and are selfish, and that's a bad formula, because new guys don't have the example," Harbaugh told the *Chicago Tribune* in 1999.

Harbaugh grew up in a competitive family, and his genes helped supply his own gotta-win outlook. Even if Harbaugh comes off more mellow publicly than those two bulging-veins coaches he cited, he said he is really one of them.

"My nature is very emotional," Harbaugh said. "I was an emotional type of player; and I'm an emotional type of coach. I just feel so strongly that football is a game of emotion, and that it's played and coached by men who are emotional.

"It's a fiery and combative game, and it takes a lot of courage for people to play it. It's an emotional game. That's just who I am, and many coaches I've played for and been around were those types of people. So I just let it come out. I just be myself and coach in that kind of vein, however you would say it."

One thing Harbaugh laments somewhat is not being able to come to Chicago very often. Now that he has his own program and lives in California, he rarely makes it back for visits. He hopes to have more chances in the future, but being a football coach tends to fill the autumn months rather thoroughly. When he thinks about Chicago and coming to the city as a young man, Harbaugh feels only warmth for the community, his Bears experiences and the lessons he learned.

"It remains my favorite big city," Harbaugh said. "I get back every now and then, but not much. I love Chicago and still have a lot of friends there, but my path has kind of taken me away. But that's the team that drafted me, that's the team I played for the longest, and Chicago and the Bears are really rich in memories for me."

25

DAN JIGGETTS

Dan Jiggetts had every reason to wonder if college football recruiters would discover him. And there was even more reason for him to wonder if the pros would track him down in college. Yet he had self-confidence in his ability as a football player and never doubted himself. Scouts of both types found him and steered him where he could play ball.

Jiggetts' high school, Westhampton Beach in New York, had only about 450 kids in grades seven through 12. He played his college football at Harvard and became a rare Ivy Leaguer chosen in the NFL draft.

"It was the same thing when I was coming out of high school," said Jiggetts, who joined the Bears for the 1976 season as an offensive lineman. "I got recruited by every football power in the country. If you can play, they'll find you. And that's what happened to me in high school and college. I was All-America in college in NCAA Division I. We were Division I just like everybody else. There wasn't I-AA yet. I had a pretty good idea I could play. I just thought I would end up on the East Coast. The father of one of my buddies in school partly owned the Jets. Strangely, one of my college roommates my senior year was from Chicago."

Jiggetts stayed home on the day of the NFL draft, waiting to be plucked, waiting to be telephoned. Round by round passed, and he was giving up.

"I was getting up and getting ready to go out because I hadn't been drafted," Jiggetts said. "As I reached the door, the phone rang, and it was the Bears. They informed me that they had drafted me in the sixth round. I was excited about that, but I said, 'I don't know anything about Chicago.' So I asked my roommate from Chicago about it. He said, 'When you see the town, you'll absolutely love it.' And I said to him, 'If you loved it so much how come you went to school in England?'"

England?

"He went to prep school in England," Jiggetts said. "His dad was a driver for some Chicago millionaire, and the guy sent my friend John overseas to attend prep school because he was an exceptional student. In fact, when he came back he went through Harvard in three years and went on to the University of Virginia law school. Now he's a very successful attorney in Chicago."

Of course, Jiggetts' Bear teammates immediately teased him about being a brain from Harvard and being an Ivy Leaguer—all of the routine razzing likely to follow a rookie football player trying to bust into the pros from a fancy college.

"Oh, all the time they gave it to me," Jiggetts said.

But his roommate was correct. Almost as soon as Jiggetts laid eyes on the city, he fell in love with Chicago.

"My first time going around town, the one thing that made me love the place was the ride I took when we turned from Congress Parkway in the loop onto Lake Shore Drive," Jiggetts said. "Just that drive north along Lake Michigan. The lights glowing from the city at night were just beautiful. Of course you get to meet a lot of people, too. I had spoken to the Harvard Club once, even though I didn't spend any time going around then. I just loved Chicago. I fell in love with the place and never wanted to leave."

Lineman Dan Jiggetts came out of Harvard to earn a place on the Bears and fell in love with Chicago. More than two decades after retirement, Jiggetts remains on top of the Chicago sports scene with his own cable television show. *Photo by AP/WWP*

Daniel Marcellus Jiggetts was born March 10, 1954, in Brooklyn, New York. He played seven seasons for the Bears at tackle and guard, ending his career in 1982. He is 6 feet, 4 inches, and played at about 275 pounds.

"I was the biggest guy in the line back then," he said. "Today, I'd be playing fullback or tight end."

Jiggetts had no nifty statistics carrying the ball, catching the ball, or throwing the ball to document his career. He was an offensive lineman, and coaches often say that they must evaulate the films before understanding how those big guys performed. What Jiggetts has is memories of wars in the trenches during the games of his life.

November 27, 1980

THE SILVERDOME
CHICAGO BEARS 23 - DETROIT LIONS 17 (OT)
By Dan Jiggetts

It was the Thanksgiving Day game that year. We were trailing, and that was never a good thing in Detroit. Per usual, whenever we played Detroit, somehow I went from backup to starter. That time, I was suddenly the left tackle, going up against Al "Bubba" Baker, who was their pass rushing specialist.

It's never an easy thing to be called on suddenly to go and play left tackle. Left tackle is the guy who has the job to protect the quarterback's blind side. I had been playing right tackle.

Bubba always got a lot of sacks, and he got me a couple of times in that game. You feel so badly because you aren't giving your team the play it needs to win the game, and it was just circumstances that I was at that position. You find yourself playing a position you hadn't been playing when the whole country is watching because it's the only game in town during that part of the day.

It's like writing with the other hand—and it's a very difficult position to play anyway. That's why, even now, they pay left tackles more than they pay right tackles. Bubba was getting the better of me in the first half, and the Lions were getting the better of us in the first half, too.

At halftime, we decided to stop throwing the ball so much since, in Walter Payton, we had the best running back of all time. We were trailing by only a touchdown, I think, but I'll never forget, at the start of the second half, I looked up at the scoreboard and somebody in the Lions' organization thought it would be a good idea to put a comment up there that said, "Walter Who?"

We were in the huddle, and Walter goes, "Did you see that?" We all said, "Yeah, we saw that." And he proceeded to gain about 120 yards in the half. The game came down to us scoring at the end of regulation to tie it and send it into overtime. I was thinking, "Thank God we tied the game," at the end of regulation. That's because I felt responsible a great deal for what the Lions had accomplished.

We came back, and we ran the football. If you have a great rushing team, the one thing the other team doesn't want to do is take the beating you're going to deliver. During that second half, I remember throwing a big block. Walter scored, and guys were flying downfield in front of him.

It's very difficult to pass block on an emergency basis, especially at left tackle. But the one thing about run blocking is, if you can run block, it doesn't matter where you play. I was an excellent run blocker. It gave me the opportunity to stop taking a beating on the offensive line and start delivering it, of which I took full advantage.

We tied it. Then it was the quickest overtime game in the history of the National Football League to date. The Lions kicked off and our return man, David Williams, fielded it. He just brought that ball back 95 yards for a touchdown. End of the day—we're out of there. Just so fast that we didn't even have to go back out on the field and deal with any more of the Lions.

We only finished that season 7-9, but the game felt like a turning point for us as a team in figuring out what it took to win.

***

Jiggetts was an outgoing guy with a willingness and energy to talk to people in public forums. He loved being a Bear, even if it was hard to get noticed as an offensive lineman. He did a great job of making himself known in the town, however, by being generous with his time off the field. When Jiggetts wasn't blocking for the Bears, he was running interference for the club in public, talking to the Boys Club and other civic organizations.

"The Boys Club, the whole nine yards," Jiggetts said. "During the course of any given year, we would do probably anywhere from 70 to 100 appearances. We'd do two or three in a day sometimes. It was just fun. Quarterback Vince Evans would go out a lot. Guys like our kicker, Bob Thomas, used to do a lot of stuff. Safety Gary Fencik would do a lot of community service stuff.

"We'd go from one thing to the next and then go play basketball. It was great. If you look back at that time, we weren't making a lot of money compared to athletes today, so a lot of us had jobs during the off-season, too. But we felt like it was part of our football job to get out and get involved with the community, and thank goodness we did. It's nice to see guys who are playing now with charitable foundations. That covers them on that end, but still there's no substitute for getting out and shaking hands and meeting people."

Jiggetts retired after the 1982 season, and by 1985, he was a full-time radio sportscaster, an experience that helped him gain an even better feel for the pulse of the community.

"You get to figure out what's important," said Jiggetts, who now hosts his own weekday, dinner-time sports show on Comcast Cable TV. "The one thing we knew on the radio, regardless of what else was going on, was to always give the listeners some Bears. It's the same thing in the television business, I think. With baseball, you've got fans divided between Cubs fans and White Sox fans. Basketball was never quite as popular in Chicago until Michael Jordan came along. Some people thought that there was a Michael phenomenon rather than just people loving the NBA. I think we learned that it was a little bit of both because, in the years after Michael left, the Bulls did poorly, and it wasn't so much fun going to the United Center, but everybody was still doing it. The Blackhawks seemed to go down a notch a little bit every year."

In other words, Da Bears rule.

Jiggetts believes that the connection between the Bears and Chicago is so strong that it even extends into player retirement. More Bears—like him—stay in the area after their playing days are over than other teams, he thinks, and goodwill built up on the field as a player and in the community making appearances has staying power.

"There are a ton of ex-Bears here," he said. "That tells you a lot about how the community welcomes the team. When you look at the number of players who actually stay in Chicago after their playing careers are over, there's a huge number. I don't think you'll find that in a lot of NFL cities.

"It's very different for us in this town. There are guys who played for other teams who live here as well."

Although it was love at first sight when Jiggetts saw the illuminated Chicago skyline from Lake Shore Drive, he could not have predicted he would still be living in Chicago nearly 30 years later. But he truly has become a Chicagoan.

"It's home," he said. "When people ask me where I am from, I now say, 'Chicago.' Not really, but I've been in Chicago longer than I was when I was growing up in New York or going to college in Boston, or anywhere else, so it is home now."

Jiggetts also thinks that his heavy involvement with community activities, being out there, being visible, when he was a player, has linked him even tighter to Chicago, both in his own mind and in the minds of fans.

"I think it's affected things in a great way that people still identify me with the football team," Jiggetts said. "Sometimes they probably wish they could forget. Hah. But I think one of the reasons was the amount of community work some of us on the team did when we were playing.

"We made ourselves part of the community. All of these years later I still run into people and maybe you stopped by their social club, or you stopped by their school, or their church, and talked to them. It never ceases to amaze me how many people's lives you have an opportunity to touch just because you took time to go out and do those things. I'm 23 years out of the football business, though not out of the business of professional sports with my broadcasting.

"I want to see guys playing now out there doing that stuff and being involved in the community. Maybe it's not the thing they want to do with their free time, but there's a reward at the end of it, and even sometimes the reward is selfish. Maybe you get to meet some of the people who are fans and get to understand the community that you're part of."

26

ERIK KRAMER

In the hot and humid air of training camp July in 1995, before the best passing season of Erik Kramer's career, he had no idea if he was going to start a single game. There was no way to know that 1995 would bring a record-breaking autumn for Kramer, or if he would even run many plays.

A year earlier, the Bears finished 10-8, including playoffs. Circumstances dictated that Steve Walsh was the primary quarterback, taking about two-thirds of all snaps. Training camp a year later was about sorting out who was going to be the starter for the new season. Kramer won that battle.

"What the Bears had done was open up the quarterback position between us, and neither of us knew what would happen," Kramer said. "I'd come in the year before as the starter and got hurt. Steve came in and did a pretty good job. When we went to the playoffs and beat Minnesota before losing to the 49ers, Steve was kind of the sentimental favorite to come back as the starter."

Yet Coach Dave Wannstedt made no guarantees to either man. He remained open-minded, and that gave Kramer the opportunity to regain the job. It worked out well for everyone—except Walsh.

"Dave said, 'I'm going to open this up,'" Kramer said. "I think, in the Bears' minds, they wanted me to start because they had brought me in to do it the year before. But certainly nothing was a given. My salary had been cut, and I had to earn the money back with incentives in my contract through playing time. That was kind of a way to say, 'Hey, it's between you and Steve. If you want it, you'll have to earn it.' I won the job in training camp and started off pretty well right away. I won my first game against Minnesota that year."

The Bears won six of their first eight games and finished 9-7. Kramer threw more frequently than any Bears quarterback in history—more than Sid Luckman, Ed Brown, or Bill Wade, putting up all-star stats.

Despite the Bears' storied history and success, in the 86-plus years of the franchise, the Bears have had few great quarterbacks. By far, the best quarterback the Bears ever counted on was Sid Luckman. The only problem is that Luckman retired 56 years ago.

What Kramer did in 1995 was splash his name all over the Bears team record book, surpassing even Luckman's best totals. That year, Kramer set Bears records for most attempts (522), most completions (315), most yards (3,838), and most touchdowns (29), as well as going the longest stretch (174) of passes without an interception. Kramer threw 50 passes in a game against the Miami Dolphins that season without being intercepted.

"Pretty good season," Kramer said, "especially since I didn't play that much the year before. The 1995 season was definitely my best."

William Erik Kramer was born November 6, 1954, in Encino, California. He played high school football in Canoga Park, California, and then attended Pierce College, a junior college, before finishing his education at North Carolina State.

Kramer was not drafted out of college and played in the Canadian Football League. He went to training camp with the New Orleans Saints, but was cut. A sturdy 6 feet, 1 inch, and 200 pounds, Kramer moved into the NFL in 1987 with the Atlanta Falcons as a strike-replacement player. He saw limited action that year, but then played

Although injuries hampered Erik Kramer's stay with the Bears, he put up team-record numbers in 1995 with 315 completions, 3,838 yards, and 29 touchdown passes.
Photo by Jonathan Daniel/Getty Images

three seasons for the Detroit Lions before joining the Bears in 1994. Kramer played five seasons for the Bears before his career ended in 1998, and most of his professional success came in the Bears' backfield. However, he was forced to cope with debilitating injuries like a broken neck, and although he has a mellow attitude towards the Bears now, he left under bitter circumstances, waived because of the arrival of draft pick Cade McNown when he could have signed a contract elsewhere earlier. Given McNown's failed tenure, the decision turned out to be about as devastating for the Bears as it was for Kramer. But he says nice things about the team now.

"The Bears are one of the greatest franchises there is," Kramer said. "They go back the farthest. They have the most Hall of Famers. It's a long, long tradition."

Kramer is definitely part of that tradition. What might have been the best overall team achievement of the season, Kramer thought, was sweeping Minnesota. The Bears took out the Vikings in the season opener in Chicago, winning by 17 points. They knew the second game would be tougher. It was, but the Bears overcame the Vikings' determination that day, too.

October 30, 1995

THE HUBERT H. HUMPHREY METRODOME
CHICAGO BEARS 14 - MINNESOTA VIKINGS 6
By Erik Kramer

It was a Monday night game. Going to play in the Metrodome, especially on a Monday night, meant it was going to be crazy loud. We were about at the halfway point of the season, and we were 5-2. We were on a roll going in.

We had come out of training camp and hit the ground running. We felt pretty good about ourselves through the first few weeks of the season. They had a very dangerous offense. Cris Carter was one of the receivers. I remember our defense rallying a little bit early in the game when we needed it.

Late in the first half, we completed a big pass to Curtis Conway, but I didn't see the catch. At that time, the Vikings' John Randle was just about the best defensive tackle in the game. I took a seven-step drop after the snap, and just as I got rid of the ball, John Randle just knocked the bejesus out of me. I came to find out later that he went through three people. He went through the guard, the center, and the running back to get me. And it happened so quickly, it was almost as if he got back there before I did. But I got the ball off, and Curtis made a great catch.

I bit the dust, but it was worth it. I didn't see the catch, either, but our sideline was celebrating pretty good. It was a hard-hitting, tight game the whole way. We won. We beat Minnesota twice that season— beating them on the road was important. Minnesota was a very tough opponent for us.

***

More victories that season would have been nice, but Kramer's individual performance was very satisfying. He fought for the quarterback job, won it, and then played the best football of his pro career in 1995. He was in a zone, gaining confidence every week, sure he could do anything on the gridiron. He played about every minute on offense, too.

"It was great," said Kramer, who now covers pro football for Fox Sports television and lives near Los Angeles. "I took every snap that year. That was very gratifying, to be a healthy No. 1 quarterback playing through some injuries. We had a chance to win just about every game we played."

Kramer's work—he often must be at another game when the Bears are playing—means that he doesn't see as much of his old team as he would like.

"I see them when I get a chance," Kramer said. "I feel connected to the Bears in every sense, though. I've taken my son, Griffin, back to Chicago; and we've seen games."

Kramer's seasons with the Bears still retain a glow. He had a grand time, and he made some wonderful memories.

"Those years were the best," he said. "We didn't win as many games as I would have hoped, but just living in that city and being a part of the Bears' family and the team's history is something that I'll always remember, and something I was proud to be part of."

27

JERRY AZUMAH

When Jerry Azumah retreats deep into Bears territory to line up as the team's kickoff returner—or whenever he intercepts a pass or otherwise makes himself prominent in a game—the signboards around the mid-section of Soldier Field light up.

"Azooomaaah!" they read, and "Azooomaah!" the fans chant.

If that makes "Zoom" Jerry Azumah's middle name, so be it. Azumah plays more than one significant role for the present-day Bears—running back kicks and backpedaling on defense as a cornerback. Given his raw speed, his background, and several facets of his history, it would be less surprising if the man who has evolved into a Pro Bowl kickoff returner was a full-time running back.

Fans who followed Azumah's college career despite the lack of television exposure, know he was a superb runner playing at NCAA Division I-AA New Hampshire. As a senior, he won the Walter Payton Award, the division's Heisman Trophy, as the top player in the classification.

Azumah, a 5-foot-10 inch, 192-pound speedster, electrified crowds in the lesser-watched Division I-AA, putting up the type of numbers that cause pinball machines to whir. As a four-year starter,

Azumah rushed for a division-record 6,193 yards and became the first Division I-AA player to run for more than 1,000 yards in each of his four seasons. While majoring in sociology, Azumah counseled the opposition. He had two 300-yard-plus games and two five-touchdown games. His senior season alone he rushed for 2,195 yards and 22 touchdowns.

Those are the kinds of statistics that make pro scouts take a second look, regardless of competition or a player's size. Many players from smaller schools have succeeded in the NFL, and no one needed to tell the Bears that. If you already came up with a gem like Payton, you tended to be more open-minded. As it turned out, the Bears were even more open-minded than Azumah dreamed. He did not know for sure whether or not he would be drafted when he completed school in 1999, and he was happy when the Bears made him a fifth-round pick. What caught him somewhat off guard was the Bears' plans for how to use him in the lineup.

"I was a college running back, and I never thought I would be playing at the highest level doing something that I'd never done before in my life," Azumah said. "That's a bet. How much of a change was it to go to defense? It was a huge change.

"At the combine, there was some talk about me being converted to defensive back. When the Bears decided to draft me, they told me they wanted me to be a defensive back. I was open to that. I had to be. In some ways, it showed that they had a lot of confidence in me. I've always had confidence in myself. I guess in asking me to make that transition they saw something in me that other teams didn't.

"I was able to make the transition. It was tough—running straight ahead versus running backwards. It definitely paid off, though, because I became a full-time starter, and things are definitely good."

Jerry Azumah was born September 1, 1977, and he grew up in Central Massachusetts. His St. Peter Marian high school team in Worcester, Massachusetts, won three state football titles with him in

The affable Jerry Azumah came out of small-college New Hampshire to make his mark for the Bears both in the defensive backfield and as a kickoff return man. He loved to get his hands on the ball. *Photo by Jonathan Daniel/Getty Images*

the lineup; and Azumah also lettered in basketball and track. As a track and field competitor, he set school records in the 100-meter dash and the long jump.

Azumah, an All-American for New Hampshire's football team, was convinced he would make it in the National Football League as a runner whether he was drafted or not.

"I knew one day I would be a running back in the league, but the Bears had a different plan for me," he said.

By the end of October in 1999, Azumah had moved into the starting lineup on defense, although he suffered a setback with a concussion. All season, Azumah played a role on special teams, and Bears teammates voted him the rookie Brian Piccolo Award for his contributions.

Despite his talent, opportunities to showcase his abilities came a little bit slower for Azumah than they did for many other top-class athletes.

"I didn't start until my senior year of high school," Azumah said. "We were a powerhouse football team, and we won the championship of our conference every year. I was a running back; and we had great running backs in front of me, so I never really had an opportunity to play much. They were older than me, and until my senior year, I didn't get out there much. It was a matter of me being patient and continuing to work hard. That's been my motto. When opportunities present themselves, I try to take full advantage of them. Senior year, I was presented with that opportunity to go out there and start.

"I did very well, but a lot of colleges didn't know about me. They usually follow you throughout high school, and I didn't start until my senior year. I rushed for more than 1,500 yards and broke several records. But because the big schools didn't know much about me, I had a lot of small schools come after me. Then it basically came down to going to either Northeastern in Boston or the University of New Hampshire, where I went."

Those were Azumah's comparatively off-the-beaten-path, big-time football choices. For a little while, Boston College, a major program, "was in the hunt," as he put it. But the Eagles never offered a scholarship.

"They pulled out, said I wasn't good enough to play for their team," Azumah said. "I remembered that in college when I rushed for a lot of yards. I'm not good enough. After I signed a letter of intent to go to New Hampshire, some big schools started to contact me. But it was too late. I was already committed, and by then, I wanted to be a big fish in a small pond."

Azumah has just completed his sixth season with the Bears, so he hopes he hasn't yet experienced the game of his life. But in the meantime, he does have one that stands out as pretty special for all-around performance.

October 26, 2003

SOLDIER FIELD
CHICAGO BEARS 24 - DETROIT LIONS 16
By Jerry Azumah

I started the first two games on defense and actually got benched for the next three games. When I came back in I said, "You know what? I want to return the ball." The coaches said okay and gave me the opportunity.

That game I made an interception, running it back 11 yards, I made 10 tackles, and I ran a kickoff back 89 yards for a touchdown. That was my first NFL kickoff-return touchdown—definitely a big game for me. That was the game that everyone, including myself, wanted to see how I would come back from adversity. Everybody's faced with adversity at some point, and for me it came early that year because I got benched. But I came back with a vengeance. I came back on defense strong, and in the return game, I knew that if the Lions gave me the ball, I was gonna make them pay. I definitely had a chip on my shoulder.

You know, that was a pivotal game for me. Any time something bad happens, I look back at that game, a game where I can draw something from. Because I was very confident at that time. I was feeling very relaxed. I was feeling that I had a lot to prove and that I was going to prove it no matter what. And that game definitely helped me that season. That kind of lifted me and guided me towards the direction I wanted to be going. Every single opportunity that came my way, I told myself I was going to take full advantage of it, just as I always had, and it was that game that pretty much set that year off for me. Everything was working—everything was clicking.

The kickoff return was special. I remember it like it was yesterday. When they put me in as the return man, I said, "I'm gonna run this." We had a particular play where the blocking wedge goes left, and I find a hole. Then I kind of bounce to the outside and just take off. I felt like it was a moment in time when I could just take full advantage of the Lions because they had been cheating on their technique a little bit, and I picked up on it. Detroit kicked off, and it was perfect. It was right between the hash marks, high and deep. I caught the ball, and I remember saying, "Okay, this could be it."

I felt it right away. I saw the wedge form up. I'm keying off a couple of guys running down the field who I have to beat. The wedge formed, and I just started running. Once the wedge hit the Lions' line, it was like everything turned to slow motion. I saw the hole immediately, and I just ran right to it.

Actually, nobody touched me. One person almost touched me. I got to the point where I was on a sideline, and I could see this guy coming into my vision. I didn't even look at him. I just stopped on a dime. He went right in front of me, and I broke it back into the middle of the field. Nobody was expecting that. Everybody was expecting me to just go out of bounds. But I felt if I could make this one cut and get back into the middle, then it's going to the house. I cut back, jetted up field, and it seemed as if people almost stopped because they thought I was out of bounds. But our guys kept working, and I just had a full escort to the end zone.

That was a great thrill, crossing the goal line. It was a big moment. It was definitely an uplifting moment for me. It was a big score and a big win. We needed that win, too.

The interception was definitely a bonus, an exclamation point—ten tackles, too. That was just one of those games where I was feeling everything. Everything was just happening.

Then, to top off the year, I was named to the Pro Bowl as a kick returner. Kick returning was always a natural thing for me. I had done it since I was a little kid, then throughout my senior year in high school and throughout college. Having the ball in my hands is very natural to me. The Bears knew I could return kicks, but at first, we had Glyn Milburn; and he had been an all-pro returner, and there were some other guys. I think the Bears felt more comfortable letting me concentrate on learning how to be a cornerback. Then, as I said, when an opportunity presented itself, I took full advantage.

I've always enjoyed running back kicks because it's a challenge. First of all, you have 11 guys screaming down the football field at you. They're looking for one thing—the football. And the football is actually in my hands. A lot of guys ask, "How do you do that? I wouldn't do that." They think it's like a suicide mission. But there are many little techniques and things you can do to get yourself in the end zone.

You try to avoid the direct hits and such that come from the front line and the wedge—the blocking schemes. Without them, there's definitely no me. It's just one play where everybody is just full speed ahead, an opportunity for me to break the game wide open. I love that. I love that about it. Every start of the game, it's the kickoff return. And if it's a kickoff return, it's my opportunity to break the game wide open and make a statement from the start.

***

Though impossible to play football and be contact shy, Azumah plays two positions, cornerback and kick returner, where the contact can be extreme. Often, the plays aren't merely tackles, but collisions. Of course, the ultimate kickoff play is a return where there is no tackle at all.

Following Azumah's big showing, the Bears' coaches, from head coach Dick Jauron to the assistants, had a new appreciation for his skills. He went from being benched to a regular. Suddenly his playing time went from low-digit minutes to full-time minutes.

"They controlled all of that stuff," Azumah said. "But I think by them putting me into the starting lineup against the Lions, they wanted to see how I would respond. And by me responding the way I did, I think it opened up their eyes to make them say, 'You know what? The kid isn't the problem. He definitely has it in him to bounce back no matter what happens. If anything bad happens he has the courage to bounce back and he's proven it.' And I continued to do that the rest of the season."

Returning a kickoff for a touchdown has so many ramifications on morale. It may be the home team fans who get revved up, or it may be the players who do the blocking getting fresh momentum. Once Azumah broke a kick, the atmosphere changed to one where true believers felt it could happen on any kickoff at any time.

"Not a lot of kicks get run back," Azumah said. "It's a tiny percentage in every league. The NFL is the best of the best, and a lot of teams don't let it happen at all. It's definitely an attitude thing. The people who are helping me block, they have to have the same attitude I do that we can return it, that 'He can pop it at any time.'

"I don't know what the odds are each time, but they can't be very high. The year I went to the Pro Bowl, I upped the ante. I felt like I had the opportunity to score every time the ball was kicked to me. Then we had the people on the return team believing it, the people on the sidelines believing it, the people in the stands, the coaches— everybody was just believing I was getting ready to pop one. It sets a tone for the whole game."

Kick return defenses get paranoid when they face a guy who has made a long return for a score. They just don't want to be the next victim. It's embarrassing when a team scores on a 90-yard runback.

"Once the first one is broken—or once you know that you have a real good return team that can score at any given moment—it gives the blockers a lot of confidence," Azumah said. "They put pressure on themselves saying, 'You know what? I'm not going to be the one to screw this up.' That's when big plays happen. During a kickoff, you know you usually have people going to the concession stand or to use the bathroom, or stuff like that, but that wasn't the case the year I went to the Pro Bowl. They didn't want to miss out."

Watching Azumah run with the football under his arm—after an interception or on a kickoff play—makes an observer wonder just how he would fare as a regular in an NFL backfield. It was not so many years ago, after all, that he was running wild for New Hampshire. And if the guy can do it on kickoffs, well, it makes you think. Maybe before Azumah retires, he will get a shot at taking handoffs, just like he did in the good old days.

The home folks would get that many more chances to shout, "Azooomaaah!"

28

BRIAN URLACHER

As both a walking highlight film and a defensive lesson plan rolled into one, Brian Urlacher terrorizes opposing offenses with his lightning-fast reactions and remarkable abilities. In a game dominated by where the ball is located, observers often find it difficult to concentrate on other aspects of the game. An aficionado's guilty pleasure may well be spending an afternoon watching the Chicago Bears' No. 54 perform defensively. The casual fan, of course, notices when those two aspects of play collide. Given Urlacher's history, that is likely to happen about 10 times a game.

Speed and fearlessness define Urlacher's game. The 6-foot-4, 258-pound mound of granite possesses the tracking skills of a cougar—with the same killer instinct. Sometimes Urlacher will thread his way to a quarterback sack, but he is at his salivating best when chasing a ball carrier attempting to broach the line of scrimmage. What makes Urlacher the most formidable defender in the NFL is his nose for the ball and his ability to sprint to an opening and fill it. Often, he can be seen racing across half of the field to haul down a runner from behind with unmatched motivation.

Urlacher virtually arrived as a fully formed star in the 2000 season after completing his college career at the University of New Mexico.

After playing some wide receiver, free safety and even returning punts and kicks for the Lobos, Urlacher made a seemingly effortless adjustment to linebacker, earning him the NFL's defensive rookie of the year award that season.

"I did it all, man," Urlacher said of his college days following an off-season summer workout at Halas Hall. "They got that four-year scholarship money out of me, that's for sure."

Urlacher is the latest in the 50-year line of succession of great and famous Bears' middle linebackers. He follows in the cleat steps of Bill George, Dick Butkus, and Mike Singletary while creating fresh tracks that some future linebacker will someday try to fill. Six years into his National Football League career, Urlacher was already a five-time Pro Bowl invitee.

Being in on 10 or more tackles per game makes for nice statistical reading, and it certainly has enhanced Urlacher's reputation as a player who is everywhere on the gridiron. But he asserts that the sheer number of tackles made does not necessarily translate into victories.

"People don't want to look at your tackles," Urlacher said. "Tackles aren't a big deal to me. I only had about 150 tackles my second year, and we went 13-3. Our defense was the best in the league. The next year I had 214, and we were like 28th. Go figure. It doesn't correlate to success."

During the Bears' 11-5 season of 2005—when they won the National Football Conference North division—the Bears nearly had the top-rated defense in the league, and Urlacher was in on 170 tackles.

Brian Urlacher was born May 25, 1978, and he was such a dominant player at Lovington High School in New Mexico that his No. 11 jersey was retired on Brian Urlacher day in 2001. Urlacher's biggest contribution to his high school team's state championship his senior year probably came on offense, where he caught 61 passes for 15 touchdowns while adding four punt returns and two kickoff returns to his TD total. He was also an all-district basketball player.

Middle linebacker Brian Urlacher has emerged as a perennial All-Pro and become the face of the franchise in the 2000s with his knack for the big play and ability to make eye-catching tackles in the open field. *Photo by Jonathan Daniel/Getty Images*

Almost from the first moment he arrived in Chicago as a first-round draft pick in 2000, Urlacher has been a widely appreciated athlete. In recent radio and newspaper polls, fans regularly have chosen him as the most popular sports figure in the city. His intense demeanor, his blondish, bullet-cut hair, and his energy in talking about team accomplishments rather than touting his own helped Urlacher become accepted quickly.

Growing up in the Southwest—and staying in the region for college—Urlacher said he had little knowledge of Chicago before the Bears selected him.

"I knew nothing," Urlacher said. "I knew of Dick Butkus, but I wasn't a Chicago fan. I'd never been to the Midwest before. I knew it was cold, [but] that's about all I knew about the place. I didn't know anything else; and then I got here, and I loved it. I wouldn't want to be anywhere else.

"The fans have taken to me—especially my first two years in Chicago they took to me. You know, you just go out there and play and keep your mouth shut. I guess it's easy to take to you when you do that."

Urlacher singled out great team performances in choosing games of his life, and he expressed a particular fondness for the 2001 season—until 2005, the only one among his first five years with the Bears that produced a division title and a spot in the playoffs. Two of Urlacher's favorite games of all time are linked by home-overtime wins, both on Pro Bowl safety Mike Brown's interceptions.

October 28, 2001
November 4, 2001

SOLDIER FIELD
CHICAGO BEARS 37 - SAN FRANCISCO 49ERS 31 (OT)
CHICAGO BEARS 27 - CLEVELAND BROWNS 21 (OT)
By Brian Urlacher

I remember everything about the 49ers game. We were down 14-0. Their defense scored twice in that game. Our quarterback, Jim Miller, ran backwards. He fumbled, and they ran it in for a touchdown early in the game. Later, Shane Matthews threw an interception, and the 49ers ran that back 97 yards for a touchdown.

By the fourth quarter, we were down 31-16, so we hadn't played good defense. We gave up a bunch of yards. We didn't make any big plays. But we scrapped back, scoring on a touchdown pass to David Terrell with 26 seconds left. The referees had to review the catch, but they gave us the touchdown. Then we handed off to "Train," Anthony Thomas, and he scored the two-point conversion. It looked like his knee was down before he got in the end zone, but they reviewed it and gave it to us again, getting us into overtime.

It was going well then—you usually don't get two reviews in a row. Right at the beginning of overtime, the 49ers had the ball. Terrell Owens ran a slant, and Jeff Garcia's pass popped off his hands. Mike Brown caught it and ran it back 33 yards for a touchdown. That was the first time it happened. We hadn't thought we were out of the game because we had a lot of time left to come back. But to win like that? Someone joked that, from then on, we put "Mike Brown intercepts for touchdown" into the game plan. I wish it were that easy.

Then, against the Browns, I thought the game was over. Athletes almost never say that because, if there's time on the clock, you always think you have a chance to win. But it was 21-7 Browns leading, and there was like 32 seconds to go.

We were driving down the field, and Marty Booker caught a touchdown pass, making it 21-14. Then I was like, "Okay, we've just got to get the onside kick here, and we can get right back in this game." And then we got the onside kick. You have to have the ball. We got the ball about the 40-yard line; and we got off another play. We threw it into the end zone, where it was tipped, and we got another touchdown. Overtime. We were getting excited. It was jubilation. We had to compose ourselves, though, because we still had to go to overtime.

The Browns got the ball first, but they only had it for a couple of plays. We got a good rush going, and the ball got tipped as it was thrown. Mike Brown intercepted it and ran it right back for a touchdown—same thing all over again. It was just amazing to come back like that. And it was back-to-back games. I don't think that will ever happen again. The same guy did the same thing two weeks in a row in overtime. I've never seen anything like that before. First of all, you don't see that many overtime games. Then to see the same play happen two weeks in a row was just unbelievable—and we won the games.

Things were not looking good for us in that Browns game. I tell you, it was not a pretty game. We were being jerks. We were fighting with them, picking fights. We had personal fouls. We had won five in a row, and we expected to win every game. We were pushing after the play, just stupid stuff. We were frustrated because we had played so well, and to show up and not play like we wanted to play bothered us. However, we came back and did what we did because our team was a team. We had offensive plays, special teams plays, and then a big defensive play to win the game.

I experienced many emotions in the Cleveland game—from being mad during the fourth quarter because we were losing to being so happy at the end of the game. After the game, I was just ecstatic. People were running around without knowing how to act. You looked at your friends and went, "Did this just happen?" It's unbelievable. Mike Brown is such a huge playmaker for our team.

The first time, I was saying, "Man, that just happened." Then the second week, against the Browns, most of the fans had already left. They were out of there, and then we had the ones who left going berserk. We just couldn't believe it would happen twice in a row.

The Bears had finished 5-11 in 2000, and no experts were picking them to even finish .500 during the 2001 season. Yet after an opening-day loss, the team got moving. There were winning streaks of six, three, and four games. In that memorable season, Urlacher might also have played his greatest individual game.

October 7, 2001

THE GEORGIA DOME
CHICAGO BEARS 31 - ATLANTA FALCONS 3
By Brian Urlacher

I had eight tackles and an interception. I filled up every category. I caused a fumble, recovered a fumble, scored a touchdown, had a tackle for a loss, and a sack. I got NFL defensive player of the week. Personally, that was my best game of that season.

As a team, we had five or six takeaways, three interceptions, two fumble recoveries on defense, and we scored on defense. There were seven or eight sacks. Michael Vick came in at quarterback for them for the second half, and we shut him down. We just had a complete game on defense. I know that was my best statistical game of the year.

The interception was great. Chris Chandler, a future teammate, was the quarterback, and we knocked him out. We had three picks in the first half. We had sacked him a couple of times. I think he was getting used to the pressure, so we blitzed. I dropped off, and Chandler throws it right to the middle of the field. I picked his pass and ran it back 10 yards. On the fumble play for a touchdown, I actually screwed up. On the goal line, they went with the play-action fake, and my man went one way. I chased the quarterback, and our defensive end, Phillip Daniels, got a hold of him and wrestled him down. He popped the ball loose—right into my hands—and I went 90 yards for a touchdown.

It felt like forever to reach the end zone. It did. When you get the ball, you get tired, man. As a defensive player, whenever you touch the ball, you automatically get tired. Then I had to go right back out on defense. Your adrenaline gets going, and you don't think about it. I don't know what it is, but right when you touch the ball, you're tired. I ran 90 yards, and nobody was close to me, but the whole time I was looking. Mike Brown was behind me, and he was chasing me. I knew *he* wasn't going to tackle me, but I knew Vick was out there, and he's a fast guy. I wanted to make sure he didn't get me. I was looking for him the whole time, but Phillip had him on the ground. The big plays are always fun.

***

Urlacher uses the word "unbelievable" frequently when he discusses the 2001 season, probably because nobody expected the Bears to finish 13-4 and probably because, until early 2006, the spoils of that season included his only NFL playoff game.

When the Bears lost their opener that season to the defending Super Bowl-champion Baltimore Ravens, 17-6, fans were not surprised. They assumed it was the start of a same-old, same-old season. But the players were angry. They felt they could have beaten the top team in the game.

"We knew we were better than we showed," Urlacher said. "We knew we could play because we played with the defending world champs. We knew we were a good team, we just didn't get it done that day. Then the next six games, we just found a way to win every game."

The pivotal game during that period was coming back from a 10-0 deficit to the Minnesota Vikings for a 17-10 victory. That was a major confidence-builder for a team suffering with a stunted ego for a number of years.

"For the last few years, [the Vikings] had always beaten up on us," Urlacher said. "They had pounded us. Then we come back on a rainy day and beat them. They're a very talented team every year, and we beat them twice that year. You get confident about yourself. We were rolling. If we needed to make a play, we made it. If we needed to cause a fumble, we caused a fumble, or got a pick. That's the way the whole season went."

Urlacher even scored an offensive touchdown that season against the Washington Redskins where he grabbed a 27-yard pass from Brad Maynard for a score on a fake punt.

"Luckily, I caught it," Urlacher said. "That was a neat play. We practiced it all week long. It was a great throw. Brad is running the option, and that's not an easy throw when you've got a guy open. You don't want to overthrow him, but you don't want to underthrow him. He hit me, and it was a touchdown."

The dream ran out of steam in the playoffs. The Bears had home-field advantage, but the Philadelphia Eagles controlled the game, winning 33-19 to end the season.

"I thought we were going to the Super Bowl," Urlacher said. "I thought there was no doubt about it. I thought we were going to pound Philly, go up to St. Louis, beat the Rams, and then to go the Super Bowl. But we laid an egg against Philly. They came in here and pounded us. We just didn't make the plays, and that's what it came down to."

As Urlacher noted, sometimes he will fill up the entire stat sheet with a variety of defensive numbers, and he always accumulates a lot of tackles. But he thinks the most telling statistic of all, the one that overshadows all others, is turnovers.

"Takeaways are huge," Urlacher said. "I think that's the biggest stat in the game. It changes the whole momentum. In 2004, against Green Bay, we were up 7-3. They looked like they're going to score a touchdown. We caused a fumble, and Mike Brown ran it back for a touchdown. That's a 14-point swing. We're up 14-3 right there. It's a huge play in the game. It's demoralizing to turn the ball over. If you've got a good drive going, and you turn a ball over, it takes away everything you've worked for."

When he was young, Urlacher never thought he'd be a Chicago Bear, never even thought he would be a professional football player. He didn't think that far ahead.

"I just had to go to college," he explained. "When I was in college, when I started getting bigger and faster, I probably asked myself if I could play. Scouts started coming around to watch us practice, so that probably gave me the idea I could do it. I almost came out for the draft after my junior year. Thank goodness I didn't. In my senior year, I knew I was going to play."

Urlacher never foresaw receiving so much adoration from Bears fans, and he sometimes acts as if he wonders if it will last, if the town will continue to like him.

"Ask me in 10 years," he said.

In 10 years, actually, Urlacher would like to be remembered as a player who was one of the cornerstones of the Chicago Bears teams that regularly made trips to the Super Bowl. What will Chicago be like when the Bears win their first Super Bowl since 1985?

"I can't even imagine," Urlacher said. "I talked to people about the 1985 Bears and what it was like after they won. I can't even imagine what the fans would do now. It would probably be bigger because it's been 20 years.

"If we get one pretty soon, I think it could be crazy."

New Year's Eve crazy—only the party might last longer than the new year.

29

TOM WADDLE

Tom Waddle grew up in Cincinnati with the goal of becoming a Major League baseball player. But football became his main game and Waddle became a star at Boston College, where he set school records. In his finest collegiate season he caught 70 passes. He also caught 13 passes in one game against Notre Dame.

For all of his accomplishments, however, Waddle, who was born February 20, 1967, was not drafted by an NFL team, perhaps because he stood just 6 feet tall and weighed 185 pounds. Waddle was noted for his perseverance and hard work, however, and caught the eye of the Bears. Signed as a free agent, Waddle tried to make the Bears' roster in 1989 and 1990, but made few appearances and spent most of his time on the team's practice squad.

Waddle showed enough to be invited to Bears training camp again in 1991 and he believed he played very well. The challenge for a player in Waddle's situation was to be significantly better than a player with a longer term contract or someone whom the coaching staff committed to with its heart and soul.

"I had worked so hard at every level," Waddle said. "I was an undrafted free agent, but I always believed in myself."

Yet Waddle was dropped from the roster again—or was about to be. On cut-down day, Waddle was ordered to Coach Mike Ditka's office for a make-or-break conversation, and the young wide receiver thought he knew which way the wind was blowing. However, Ditka's actual comments caught him off-guard.

In a somewhat bizarre conversation that Waddle remembers very well, Ditka informed him he was going to be released again so the team could meet the roster requirements under league rules. Then he would be re-signed and would suit up in the 1991 season opener against the Minnesota Vikings that weekend.

"By that time I was kind of calloused to what was going to be said," Waddle said. "Then he said, 'But you're going to be dressed for opening day.' I looked at him in shock. He also said, 'You're not going to play.' That was his honesty, but frankly that was one of the things I liked about him."

Waddle was released, went home, came back the next day and was re-signed as pretty much the last man on the team. Then on Sunday he put on a Bears uniform for what he thought might be the last time. Once the game clock began ticking and the Bears weren't moving the ball, things changed.

September 1, 1991

SOLDIER FIELD
CHICAGO BEARS 10 - MINNESOTA VIKINGS 6
By Tom Waddle

The receiver starters were Glen Kozlowski, Ron Morris and Dennis Gentry. Jim Harbaugh was the quarterback.

All of a sudden I got put in the game. It was a close game all of the way without too much scoring. I never thought I would get the ball. A play was called and I ran my route. I can remember getting behind the cornerback and I didn't think anyone else was around who could get me.

I remember turning around at about the 16-yard-line and being shocked. There was the ball. I caught it, ran across the goal-line for a touchdown, and as I went down forward, with the ball in front of me, both of my elbows went into my stomach and it knocked the wind out of me. I was thinking, "My goodness, am I going to die here for lack of oxygen?"

Everyone was celebrating, but I wasn't. Nobody understood that I couldn't because I couldn't breathe. I got a 37-yard touchdown pass and that gave us a 7-3 lead.

We won the game and that was the winning touchdown. It was huge. The reaction was huge, too. There was a front-page picture in the *Chicago Tribune* of me catching the ball. If I don't make that catch I probably don't have a career.

***

Overnight, Waddle, who made another catch for 11 yards in the victory before 64,112 fans, was transformed from a guy on his way out the door to a starting player who caught 55 passes that season for an 11-5 Bears team, earning his coach's trust and confidence.

He overcame the stigma of being too small and not having track sprinter speed.

"You do have physical limitations," Waddle said. "It's all about speed and size. I was as quick as anyone on our team side-to-side."

Waddle also had seasons of 46 and 44 catches for the Bears and he occasionally ran back punts and kickoffs. At the end of his NFL career Waddle was property of the Cincinnati Bengals, but did not appear in a game for his hometown team.

Although Waddle jokes that he did not have "blinding speed" at least in one game against the Atlanta Falcons he apparently fooled super-fast defensive back Deion Sanders when he scored on him.

"I have a picture of Deion Sanders diving at my feet," said Waddle, who made 173 catches for nine touchdowns in six pro seasons. "He said, 'Dude, you're the best white wide receiver I've ever played against.'"

Waddle said he considered that to be a cool compliment until one of his teammates pointed out the comparative shortage of white wide receivers by noting, "There's Ricky Proehl, Ed McCaffrey and you."

Waddle, who lives in a Chicago suburb with his wife and four daughters, said "I was blessed" to have an NFL career at all. Currently, he is a full-time sportscaster, co-host of a popular morning sports talk radio show in Chicago called "Waddle and Silvvy." He also handles several other broadcast duties, including work for the NFL Network.

30

ALEX BROWN

Alex Brown was born in tiny Jasper, Florida, a community of less than 2,000 people, but there was nothing tiny about him. Brown grew up to become a king-sized defensive lineman, first for the University of Florida, and then the Bears.

Of all things, Brown was a quarterback in high school for the Hamilton County Trojans, though he also doubled as a linebacker. As a senior in high school Brown was a dominant player with 117 tackles, five blocked passes and four fumble recoveries. He was a terror on the defensive side of the ball, a game changer.

Brown was born June 4, 1979, and he was such a sensation that Gator recruiters could hardly miss him. The real question was the best position for a player who grew to 6-foot-3 and 260 pounds. Instead of remaining a quarterback, Brown became expert at chasing them.

Those were the Steve Spurrier days in Gainesville and Brown became an integral part of the Gator defense. Twice between 1999 and 2001 Brown was chosen as a first-team All-American. A three-time Southeastern Conference all-star, Brown was also the league's defensive player of the year in 2001.

The traits that established Brown as a first-rate National Football League defensive end emerged in college. One season he collected 13 sacks, and Brown still owns the Florida career mark of 33 sacks. Brown routinely snacked on quarterbacks.

Taken in the fourth round (the 104th player chosen) of the 2002 NFL draft, Brown was stunned and disappointed that he had dropped so low. The anger he felt at the disrespect helped fuel his success with the Bears.

Right from the start in his 2002-2009 Bears career, Brown demonstrated that every team in the league that passed on him coming out of college had made a mistake.

"I was not happy about going in the fourth round," Brown recalled years later. "I thought I was better than that. I was happy to be drafted by the Bears because I thought they were a good team. I was glad they took me, but the main thing I thought about Chicago was it was cold as heck."

February 4, 2007

DOLPHIN STADIUM
INDIANAPOLIS COLTS 29 - CHICAGO BEARS 17
By Alex Brown

Although we lost Super Bowl XLI to Indianapolis, that game stands out as the game of my life. It was something I always dreamed of seeing and being a part of from the time I started playing football. The biggest thrill for me was when I realized we were going. There was about four minutes left in our playoff game against the New Orleans Saints.

I had that electrical charge come across my body. After all of this time and hard work you're being rewarded with the trip to the Super Bowl. That was one of the most amazing moments in my NFL career. Just the realization, "We are going."

I was standing on the sideline and Ian Scott (another Bears defender) actually came up to me and said it. It was the realization after a Thomas Jones touchdown that they (the Saints) can't come back. They're done. We had a good season. We were 13-3. You think you can reach the Super Bowl, but it wasn't until that moment that it became real. It was the first time I sat back knowing we were going to it.

On the day of the game itself, inside the stadium, I just soaked it all in. I remember all of the stuff from before the game. They announce the lineups. All of the flashbulbs go off in the stands. But when all of the smoke clears it's just football.

It was a great game. We got to see history made when Devin Hester ran back the opening kickoff (92 yards for a touchdown). It's the first play, just seconds into the game, and you are feeling really good. We felt even better then. After that (a 7-0 lead), you've got to stay focused.

It was two really good teams playing and only one could be crowned a champion. They were able to put together more plays than we did on that day. I thought we were the better team with our defense and our running game. But they had Peyton Manning at quarterback and we couldn't put a lot of pressure on him as a team.

***

The game was played in the rain and the climate seemed helpful to the Bears' strengths; but the Colts had complete dominance in time of possession, controlling the ball for more than 38 minutes to the Bears' 21-plus.

Brown was in on two tackles.

The Bears seemed to be a team on the rise and as soon as the loss was catalogued they started thinking about getting back to the Super Bowl the next season. But minor personnel changes added up to a lot, changing the depth and chemistry of the club. Chicago finished 7-9 in 2007 and did not qualify for the playoffs.

"In training camp the next year we began to realize it was not the same team," Brown said. "There had been some changes. The reason we were so good before was that we had backups who could come in and play like starters. They went to other teams. You had to have guys who were unselfish, players on special teams that would sacrifice."

The Bears did not return to the Super Bowl for the rest of Brown's stay with the team, but when he retired after a season with the Saints in 2010, he made his home in the Chicago suburbs.

"In Chicago, people loved to watch the defense," Brown said. "They'll forget us, though, because we didn't win it all. I really thought we were good enough to be talked about with that 1985 team (the only Bears Super Bowl champion squad). We had really good players at every position."

Brown operates his own logistics business and during the football season he works as a broadcaster for outlets such as Comcast and NBC.

"Football was a great part of my life," Brown said. "But that's what it was, a part. I don't regret anything. I played nine years and never missed a game. For nine years I played as hard as I could. I didn't want to say 'I wish I had…' I wish we won the Super Bowl, though."

31

DESMOND CLARK

By the standards of many professional football players Desmond Clark was a late bloomer. He was born April 20, 1977, in Bartow, Florida, and it was not until he was attending Wake Forest of the Atlantic Coast Conference that he first entertained the idea that he might have the skills to make a living playing the game.

"I wasn't dreaming of it in college," Clark said. "I was just trying to be the best player I could be."

Clark, who at 6-foot-3 had a playing weight of about 250 pounds, was a tight end with the Bears, but also spent time during his career as a fullback and a long snapper for kicks. Clark became a polished receiver in college where he made 216 receptions for 20 touchdowns. His yards per catch average 13.2.

The Denver Broncos saw something in Clark and made him their sixth-round draft pick in 1999. Being noticed excited Clark and so did being selected by the Broncos. Behind quarterback John Elway Denver was a two-time defending Super Bowl champ and Clark believed he was walking right onto a roster where he could immediately win a Super Bowl ring.

"Super Bowl here we go," Clark recalled thinking. "'I'll be going to a Super Bowl, too."

Not quite. Clark was a year late. He was also about a year early in making a mark. During his rookie season with the Broncos Clark rarely saw the ball, making just one catch. But Clark nabbed 27 balls his second season and 51 his third year.

The 2002 season was pretty much a lost year with the Miami Dolphins, but the highlights of Clark's career lay ahead when he joined the Bears in 2004. It was at the end of the 2006 season, when the Bears finished 13-3, that Clark's Super Bowl goal was fulfilled when the team met the Indianapolis Colts.

February 4, 2007

DOLPHIN STADIUM
INDIANAPOLIS COLTS 29 - CHICAGO BEARS 17
By Desmond Clark

The Super Bowl would be my favorite game even though we lost. That's the one when I'm old and gray that I'll remember best. As a kid that's what you want to do. You sit in front of the TV set and you picture playing in it. Everyone's eyes are focused on you. There's not a whole lot of people that can say they went to the Super Bowl.

It's unbelievable. When you go out on the field, it's something that you have to be there to comprehend. It's the grandest game of them all. I had to calm myself down on the sideline after we got introduced and the crowd was cheering and the cameras were flashing.

Everything leading up to it reminds you "This is not a regular game." I was taking in all that stuff. I was thinking, "I'm proud to be playing in the Super Bowl" I just wanted to take it all in. I was talking to myself. I told myself, "It's the same game. Just go out and play."

The game began with Devin Hester's kickoff return (a 92-yard touchdown). Now you're like, "Gee, you can't have a better start than that." I had to calm myself down again. We couldn't have a better start. Now we're on our way. Once I got into the game it was just business as usual.

After that first possession it was a football game. The rain, that part was lousy, but everyone had to deal with it. I think my best play in the game was throwing a block that sprung Thomas Jones for like a 36-yard gain.

In the fourth quarter when we got behind, I was catching a lot of balls from quarterback Rex Grossman. They weren't big plays. It was one of those things where we were moving the ball. Quick passes, not deep passes. I caught four on our last drive. I caught six passes in the game, but you want to make those six catches count for a little more (than 64 yards with a long of 18).

That year I had one of my best games against the Tampa Bay Bucs. I made seven catches. Me and Rex had a pretty good connection going. We made some big plays. As soon as I broke off a route and turned, the ball was already in there.

In the Super Bowl, everything was a dump-off pass, up and under every time. When I caught the ball I had three or four people around me every time. There was no chance to break anything longer. That's what the Colts defense was playing for. On the last play of the game the ball was thrown deeper, but the play was broken up.

I thought the rain would be to our advantage because of our running game and defense and the Colts relied on the pass, but that didn't happen.

When the game ended I was devastated. My college coach Jim Caldwell was on the other sideline. All of the confetti was falling and they were celebrating. That was a depressing feeling.

***

Getting to the Super Bowl was wonderful, but coming out of the Super Bowl with an L rather than a W was hard for Clark to stomach.

"It took me a couple of months to watch that game," Clark said. "And I watched it once."

Clark felt the Bears could make a quick return to the Super Bowl and maybe win it the next season, but all of the things that broke right for the team in 2006 went against the Bears in 2007.

Clark played in the NFL from 1999 through 2010 and he retired with 323 receptions for 3,591 yards and 27 touchdowns.

After his playing days Clark, who earned his college degree in communications, stayed in the Chicago area and became a realtor and a radio personality. For a time he and ex-Bears teammate Alex Brown shared a local radio show, but now Clark co-hosts a different show.

Around town Clark is well-remembered from his Bears playing days.

"It is a help to me," Clark said. "That's how everybody in Chicago knows me, through the Bears."